MALÖRT

THE
REDEMPTION
 OF A
REVERED &
REVILED SPIRIT

JOSH
NOEL

CHICAGO
REVIEW
PRESS

Copyright © 2024 by Josh Noel
All rights reserved
Published by Chicago Review Press Incorporated
814 North Franklin Street
Chicago, Illinois 60610
ISBN 978-0-914091-67-7

Library of Congress Control Number: 2024939915

Cover design and typesetting: Jonathan Hahn

Printed in the United States of America

To Evan and Abby—
one day I'll give you a taste of Malört.
Hopefully you'll forgive me.

CONTENTS

PROLOGUE

MALÖRT IS A punch line. An endless punch line.

It has been described as tasting like "a forest fire, if the forest was made of earwax" and "burnt vinyl car-seat condensation." It has been called "hairspray and death," akin to "swallowing a burnt condom full of gas."

The actor and writer John Hodgman famously said Malört tastes like "pencil shavings and heartbreak," as if flavored with "darkness and pain." Hodgman would bring a bottle to his stage shows, take a swig, send the bottle around the room to an unsuspecting (and soon to be horrified) audience, then drink from it once again. He'd brag the stunt never made him sick; whatever was in Malört killed every germ.

The helpless, pained contortion that accompanies a first taste of Malört is affectionately, or maybe not so affectionately, known as "Malört face." The shock and brutality are immortalized in countless photos and videos across the internet.

More than one journalist has turned to Malört for a quick and amusing tale—"10 Top New York Sommeliers Try Malört"—where the punch lines write themselves: "It's making me grind my teeth, as if I'd had 26 shots of espresso."

Writers have long wrestled with Malört's allure, whether sneering ("Malört is the Worst Booze Ever. And You Need to Try It"), diplomatic ("Why This Off-Putting Chicago Novelty Liquor Is So Damn Special"), or quizzical ("Malört: Sin Against God or Actually, Kinda Good?").

Yet lurking in the horror and the mockery lies the truth of Malört, and one of those New York sommeliers stumbled upon it: "This is actually painful both to smell and taste, so bad that I keep going back, hoping to see if it gets better!"

The truth is this: We keep going back. For nearly a hundred years, we've gone back.

In a car heading home from the airport one fall afternoon in 2022, I asked my driver, a friendly guy in his early thirties named Jordan, a question: "Have you heard of Malört?"

His response was swift and emphatic: "It's the worst liquor I've ever had." Then, as we zipped along Chicago's Kennedy Expressway in Jordan's maroon RAV4, he told a story.

The first thing he legally drank in a bar, surrounded by friends on his twenty-first birthday, was a shot of Malört. His pals took him out, and the bartender didn't hesitate to do what a Chicago bartender does: he handed Jordan a rite-of-passage shot of Malört—on the house, of course. Jordan slugged it down. His friends cheered. And then he understood: the shock, the horror . . . the fascination.

Now Jordan shares the wisdom. When he's driving tourists, especially younger visitors asking about bars to check out, he makes a point of urging them to try Malört. He doesn't say much more than that. He wants them to discover it as he did. For better, for worse.

Like so many first tastes of Malört, mine, like Jordan's, came by happenstance. Some friends and I were going out, and one of them charged me with finding a bar for the evening. The one mandate: it had to serve Malört. I'd never heard of it. It was some kind of weird, terrible liquor, I was told.

I wondered why we would want to drink such a thing, but I dutifully called around, asking quizzically, "Do you have something called Malört?"

We wound up at a recently opened cocktail bar called the Whistler. We ordered our shots. My reaction was unequivocal.

What the fuck is that?

I found Malört equal parts strange and interesting, though mostly I was confused. It was jarringly bitter and astringent—like a mouthful of rubber bands marinated in grapefruit peel and rubbing alcohol—and the sharp-elbowed aftertaste seemed to linger interminably. I rarely thought about it much again. For a while.

During the next few years, Malört's fame, and infamy, grew—first in Chicago, then slowly beyond. At the same time, my role at the *Chicago Tribune* morphed from news writer to travel writer to covering Chicago's quickly changing drinking landscape. A city without a single brewery or distillery in the mid-1980s became home to plenty of both, and my job was to chronicle that change. Yet, of all the subjects I covered—breweries, bars, visionary beers, meticulously layered cocktails—few things resonated like Malört.

Yes, it was weird and unpleasant to most taste buds. But—and with Malört, there's always a *but*—it was like nothing else. It made no sense: a strange, bitter Swedish spirit available only in Chicago. Everyone seemed to wonder, as I did, *What the fuck is that?* And even more so: *Why does it exist?*

Its reputation and its lore became its charm, generating power no marketing team could hatch around a conference table: *I love this thing and I hate this thing, and I love to hate this thing. I want you to try it so that you can love to hate it with me—and maybe even love it.* Few people taste Malört for the first time and say, *Hey, that's good!* Instead, like for Jordan, that first taste is more likely to bring astonishment and a story to tell for all time.

This is the story behind those stories.

———————

Malört could have died a hundred deaths during the last hundred years. Its survival wasn't always a given. It also was no accident.

There was one man's dogged persistence. One woman's patience and dedication. There were cultural shifts and fortunate timing. And there has been *you*. The drinker.

After decades as an odd afterthought, a new generation not only came to understand Malört—it decided Malört was cool. The same tastes that embraced the ideas of "craft," "local," and "farm to table" found

1

GEORGE AND PAT

THE AD SAT at the bottom of the fifth column on page D34 of the Sunday paper, below the heading HELP WANTED—WOMEN/STORES AND OFFICES.

SECRETARY
Loop law and business office. Shorthand essential. Rapid typing required.
Attractive surroundings for girl working alone—responsible to one executive.
DE2-3772   Mr. Brode

Pat Gabelick circled the ad as she picked through the *Chicago Tribune* that wintry morning in 1966, at the suburban home she shared with her mother. She knew she was qualified.

Pat was twenty-three, a working-class girl from Cicero, a town along Chicago's western edge packed with factory workers and mafiosi. Her first job after high school was at an architecture firm in downtown Chicago, as secretary to one of the vice presidents. Her boss tested her shorthand during the interview by talking at a normal speed, then increasingly quickly. Pat kept up, no problem.

That skill was the rare good thing to come from high school. Pat learned to bang out 120 words a minute and scratch furious notes.

Morton East High otherwise felt like a trite and confining four years, something that existed only to move past. When she was done, Pat never wanted to see the inside of a classroom again.

Most girls Pat knew planned to go to college or to marry as soon as they could. Neither was for Pat. She was ready for adulthood—to make her own money, live on her own, socialize in the bars, flirt with some boys. She'd settle down eventually, have kids, and tend to the house. Until then, she'd enjoy herself, especially in those bars after work. Her first drink was at sixteen, at a Christmas party hosted by the savings and loan where she worked part-time. Rows of martinis and Manhattans lined the bar, and when no one seemed to be looking, she grabbed a Manhattan. She put the sweet, boozy rush to her lips. She was sold.

Weeks after graduating high school, Pat began commuting to downtown Chicago's clatter and hustle, earning seventy-five dollars a week.

She stayed in the job four years, until her family moved to a suburb ten miles farther out. Pat went to work for a bank close to her new

Pat Gabelick at the age
of nineteen in 1962.
Courtesy of Pat Gabelick

home, again working as a secretary for a vice president. She quickly grew bored. She felt too young to be in the suburbs all day. She wanted to be back downtown, back in the action. She briefly took a job at Automatic Canteen, a company that made vending machines, but that didn't work out. So here she was, looking again.

Pat called the number. She asked for Mr. Brode.

George Brode told Pat about the job. He was a lawyer, he said, representing business interests, mostly. He worked alone. It would be just the two of them.

A small office didn't appeal to Pat, but the location did: 201 North Wells Street, a twenty-eight-story skyscraper also home to the architecture firm where she worked months earlier. She already knew plenty of people in the building and would have ready lunch dates and postwork drinking companions. She and Mr. Brode agreed to an interview.

Their meeting didn't instill much more enthusiasm for the job. George's fourteenth-floor office was dim and dated, wood paneling affixed

George Brode, fifty-nine, in his downtown Chicago office in 1969.
Courtesy of Pat Gabelick

2

A YEAR AND A DAY

THE LIQUOR BUSINESS was good to George. At least for a while.

Through the 1930s, a post-Prohibition thirst reenergized the spirits industry. Bielzoff Products ramped back up with its dozens of products, chronicled in thick, handsome catalogs George handed out during his weeks on the road, bouncing between Denver, Los Angeles, San Francisco, New Orleans, and cities along the East Coast.

It was a lucrative few years for George that became only more so after the 1941 bombing of Pearl Harbor. As the federal government conscripted American distilleries to shift production to nonconsumable, high-proof alcohol for the War Production Board—to make plastics, rubber, textiles, gunpowder, glass, fuel, antifreeze, and explosives—any company still selling spirits sat on a gold mine. That included Bielzoff Products.

Bielzoff didn't distill its own liquor; it bought vodka, whiskey, and gin in massive quantities, infused flavors and syrups as needed, packaged its products, and sent them into the market. Even as war raged, Bielzoff was well stocked for years of production. George Broide became a rich man.

He used his wealth to dive deeper into the industry. In 1943 he bought a stake in Belle Meade Distillery in northeastern Virginia, known for its whiskey before shifting to production of synthetic rubber for the war. George became a vice president of the company. Two years later, as the war wound down, he bought Bielzoff Products, a deal that earned a brief

George Brode's 1930s headshot as a young Bielzoff
Products executive. *Courtesy of Pat Gabelick*

write-up in the *Chicago Tribune* and "involved several million dollars," the newspaper reported.

More than once, Fritzi expressed her disappointment at the turn their lives had taken. She thought she was marrying a lawyer, she told her husband, not a liquor baron. But the quality of the lifestyle was undeniable.

In 1946 the Broides joined a postwar exodus of Jewish Chicagoans who traded the city for the leafy, quiet northern suburbs. George spent $45,000 to build a six-bedroom house a block from Lake Michigan in the village of Glencoe, one of the few suburbs to welcome Jews at the time. The year they moved into the house, George and Fritzi welcomed their third and final child, a son named David.

George's rise into society's upper crust came to a swift end on a Tuesday morning that December, when the seemingly law-abiding, rags-to-riches liquor mogul was indicted by the US Justice Department. The charge: draft evasion.

Federal prosecutors alleged George's stake in Belle Meade was in fact shirking his eligibility for the draft, and that he lied to his local draft board about his role in the company. When American men between twenty and forty-four were liable for military service, George, who was thirty-three, attested that he took a pay cut from his lucrative career at Bielzoff to manage Belle Meade's rubber production for the War Production Board at a lower middle-class salary of $2,500 a year.

"I handle the priorities and maintenance of distillery plant," he told Local Selective Service Board No. 77 on Dec. 3, 1943. "Also handle the purchases of grain for distillation of government war alcohol and in charge of contractual relations with W.P.B."

He told the board he had just returned from "an important trip" to Louisiana to inspect rubber production.

In reality, prosecutors alleged, George continued operating Bielzoff Products at a salary of more than $50,000 a year. He was among the nation's top one percent of earners.

His attorney filed a motion to dismiss the charge in February 1947, arguing the indictment failed to "state facts sufficient to constitute an offense against the United States." Judge Philip L. Sullivan denied the motion. George pleaded not guilty.

At trial three months later, prosecutors laid out their case: George secured a deferment early in the war, claiming enlistment would be a hardship on his young family. Worried he might lose his deferral status as the battle wore on, he bought five thousand shares of Belle Meade and became a vice president solely to mislead the draft board.

The allegation was supported by dozens of witnesses, years of Belle Meade's corporate documents, reams of George's correspondence, and a painstaking recreation of his movements, bolstered by hotel records: a month in California in October 1943; two weeks in New Orleans a month later; ten days in Los Angeles in March 1944, followed by five days in Denver; back to Denver in September, then another two-week trip to Los Angeles and up to San Francisco; and nearly a month in Los Angeles in spring 1945, again followed by a visit to San Francisco.

Prosecutors even subpoenaed a photograph and its negative from a January 1945 sales meeting in Denver "showing persons present standing in front of a large outdoor sign" advertising Bielzoff Products, an image the FBI turned up during its investigation.

Prosecutors asked the judge to sentence George to a year and a day in prison.

George and his attorney were likely surprised at the prosecutors' appetite for a fight. They also probably doubted he would get much in the way of punishment. The war had been over nearly two years. George was a productive and respected member of society. He was a lawyer. A father of three.

He changed his plea to guilty, gambling on the judge's sympathies. His lawyer choked up as he pleaded for clemency, asking for George's chance to "make his contributions to society." Otherwise, he said, George's life would be in shambles.

The argument, and any assumptions about the judge's leaning, backfired.

"What makes this more serious than the ordinary case under the ordinary circumstances is the education of this defendant, plus the fact that he is a lawyer," Judge Sullivan told the court. "Now, if this was a truck driver, that would be one thing, and he probably would not get any consideration at all. I think the recommendation of the government is very fair, and I am going to follow it. A year and a day."

George burst into sobs.

News of his conviction anchored the front page of the next morning's *Chicago Tribune*, below the headline GLENCOE DRAFT EVADER GETS YEAR IN PRISON.

> A wealthy Glencoe resident, head of a large liquor company and an officer in several other companies, was sentenced to a year and a day in prison by Federal Judge Philip L. Sullivan yesterday after he pleaded guilty to a charge of draft evasion.
>
> He is George Broide, 36, president of the D.J. Bielzoff Products company, 1109 S. State St., a manufacturer of

cordials and liquors. Broide, who is also an attorney, lives
with his wife and three young children at 175 Park Av. in
the suburb.

A small photo of George accompanied the article. He wore large round
glasses and a tie, his mouth slightly agape in what looks like a moment
of despondence, desperation, or, quite likely, both.

———————————

George arrived at the federal prison in Terre Haute, Indiana, on a typically warm and muggy central Indiana summer day in June 1947. The
medium-security prison had opened just seven years earlier, a few miles
east of the Illinois border and two hundred miles due south of the idyllic
suburban home George had left behind.

George was among the wealthiest and most educated prisoners in Terre
Haute, and he developed a quick reputation as helpful and cooperative.
He took a job in the prison library and taught other inmates to read.

He became eligible for parole after just four months, appearing before
the board on November 19, 1947. He said he learned his lesson and was
committed to doing better. He was humbled and ready to return to his
life and family. The board approved his release for December 3—a year
since his indictment.

For reasons lost to time, George wound up leaving just five days later,
on the Monday before Thanksgiving. He spent 164 days in federal prison.

———————————

Back home, George's prison time was not to be discussed. Everyone
knew as much.

His youngest son, David, a toddler when George went to Terre Haute,
only learned it had happened twenty years later, while home from college
and shooting pool with his uncle in a dive bar on Chicago's North Side.
The revelation floored David, not only the fact of it but also that it was
kept from him for so long. His mother never told him. His siblings never
told him. George's conviction, he realized, was a quiet shame hanging
over the family.

David asked his mother about it. She told him, yes, it happened, but his father knew it was a mistake, the punishment was brief, and George did right by tutoring fellow inmates. George didn't embarrass easily, but David knew not to ask about it. The question would have enraged him.

George was discharged from parole on June 13, 1948, a year to the day after arriving in Terre Haute. The episode changed him. It sapped some of his joy, muted his optimism. He was never carefree or emotive, but after prison he only became more reserved—often polite but rarely kind, an introvert who went to bed early and woke up before sunrise. He was a remote parent, more likely to talk *at* his children than with them. He adored his daughter but never grew close to his sons. They saw him as a loner, most interested in finding a quiet room to read or watch TV.

After prison, George looked to start anew. He changed the family name to "Brode"—the way it was pronounced. He changed the name of his business too, from Bielzoff Products to Red Horse Liquors, for the company's popular Red Horse line of spirits. Red Horse Liquors didn't last long—only until 1953, when George returned to practicing law.

The reason was rooted in a miscalculation about the Korean War. As George knew well, World War II upended the distilling industry, sapping the nation of its spirits production. George envisioned a similar scenario unfolding during the Korean War.

That conflict began in June 1950, and within a month, the United States, United Nations, and China were embroiled in the fight. Should the nation be on the verge of World War III, whiskey would again become scarce. George bought massive stocks of whiskey, imagining distilleries would again be mobilized to support the effort.

But barely a tenth of the American soldiers who fought in World War II went to Korea, and the conflict resolved in three years. Distilleries weren't called upon to support the war as they did in the 1940s. George gambled—and he lost. He had no choice but to sell Red Horse Liquors, which he did on May 1, 1953, to a local competitor, Union Liquor Company, for $62,500, to be paid over ten years—less than the value of his house. A decade earlier, before his prison stint, the business was valued at more than $800,000.

Red Horse Liquors distributor price list, early 1950s, which included Jeppson's Malört among many other products. By 1953, George Brode would sell all but one: Jeppson's Malört. *Courtesy of Peter Strom*

Fritzi used the episode as a warning to her children for years to come. Don't put all your eggs in one basket, she said. Don't make the mistake your father did.

George was fortunate to have a law degree in reserve, but there was a problem: he had been disbarred after his conviction, in September 1947. His only hope was a pardon from President Harry S. Truman. George was a reliable Republican voter—the type who believed *he* had worked his way up from nothing, so everyone else could too—but turned to the Missouri Democrat for a chance to start fresh.

On April 28, 1952, George got his pardon, full and unconditional, signed by the president himself, who noted George had "conducted himself in a law-abiding manner" since his conviction. On March 27, 1953, George was reinstated to the Illinois bar.

George soon launched his legal practice at 201 North Wells Street. Before leaving his Red Horse office, a mile and a half south, he pried the wood paneling from the walls and the red leather-bound door from its hinges, to be reinstalled in his law office. He also took a single brand from the Red Horse catalog: that bitter liquor Carl Jeppson sold to him nearly twenty years earlier.

Even before selling Red Horse, George renamed what Carl likely called Jeppson's Malörtbrännvin—"Jeppson's wormwood liquor"—and plugged it into the Bielzoff visual identity with a pale yellow-green label that appeared to be peeling at the edges, adorned with an elaborate crest: three five-pointed stars angled on a white stripe hugged by pale blue, sitting in a medallion of curves and lines topped with a crown.

Below was George's new name for the product, invoking the elderly Swede who sold it to him:

Jeppson's
Malört
Liqueur

Swedish Type Brännvin
Made from the imported Swedish Malort Plant
Formula of Carl Jeppson

3

THE HORNY-HANDED
MALE ARTISAN

GEORGE'S CAREER AS a liquor executive was down to one strange and polarizing product, and the way to make it thrive, as much as a strange and polarizing product could thrive, was something that had long been true in the alcohol business and would be true forever: always be selling. He did it when he owned dozens of brands, and he did it now, selling not only Jeppson's Malört but also the *idea* of Jeppson's Malört to the bartenders, the shop owners, his army of distributors, and, of course, Chicago's drinkers.

Each was a unique audience, and George had to speak to them all. At larger companies, teams of marketers and salesmen handled such strategies. At the Carl Jeppson Co.—newly formed to house Jeppson's Malört after the demise of Red Horse Liquors—George *was* the company.

He thought it particularly important to woo the customer, and it was a golden age for doing so. The economy had recovered after World War II, and a housing boom was on. Americans were feeling good. They were drinking, and drinking a lot. They were ready to spend.

The spirits industry was in the middle of a self-imposed sixty-year ban on television and radio advertising, but no matter: weekly magazines and daily newspapers reached hundreds of millions of readers. Seagram's, Johnnie Walker, and Jim Beam—which hired no less than 007 himself, Sean Connery, to cradle its bourbon—were staples of midcentury print advertising. Even the iconic charcoal-filtered Tennessee whiskey, Jack

Daniel's, after thriving for eighty years on lore and word of mouth, hired its first marketing director and began regular advertising.

George formed the Atlas Advertising Agency, whose only client was Jeppson's Malört, solely for agency discounts from Chicago's three major daily newspapers. He hired artists to draw his ads, but the words and ideas were his.

George's mid-1950s marketing approach was cautious and conventional as he wrestled with making Malört make sense to a mainstream audience. (He also began a stretch of about five years in which he dropped the word "Malört" from the name of the product, referring to it solely as "Jeppson.") He tried positioning it as a "fine liquor," appreciated by "mature" drinkers and "discriminating tastes." In one ad he compared it to, of all things, green olives:

> Remember the first time you tried green olives? I'll bet you said just as I did, "How in the world can people eat this bitter, pungent fruit; much less be wild about it?"
>
> Like me you found out. Your second green olive tasted a little better. With your third, you were hooked for life.
>
> Come to think of it—most discriminating tastes in food—olives, lobsters, oysters, watercress, clam chowder— they're all acquired tastes.
>
> And so it is with Jeppson. The taste and tang of this fine liquor is so subtly different and so unlike any other liquor in all the world . . . you actually must acquire a taste for it before all its full, rich, warming goodness is revealed to you. But then . . . ahhh . . . nothing can replace Jeppson when you seek the ultimate in relaxed imbibing.

Still not ready to tout its intense bitterness—or to declare it "bold, harsh and rugged," as he would ten years later—George embraced Malört's dryness, which he used as a springboard to invent two cocktails: the Stockholm (a Malört Manhattan) and the Pepper-Upper (a Malört martini). The Stockholm, he said in table-tent advertisements given to bar owners with the hope of catching the wandering barfly's eye, was "the world's dry-est dry Manhattan!" The Pepper-Upper was the "dryest dry martini ever served." In case either became a sensation, George trademarked both names. (He also did the same for a term he would forever attach to Malört: "two-fisted liquor.")

By the late 1950s, George had left behind the idea of Malört as "relaxed imbibing." Rather than suggest his wormwood liqueur as haute, or even enjoyable, his messaging grew zanier and cornier, fueled by the recognition that he was in fact selling an absurd product, at least to American palates.

"Start your drinking with Jeppson and . . ." read a 1957 ad, "Quitchyerbellyachin'."

> Look at it this way. You want a drink but beer, bourbon or
> berries just don't "send" you. Our suggestion: try Jeppson,
> because here for once is a truly different liquor. When the
> impact of this "starting" liquor takes hold, you will realize
> its internal possibilities. At that time you can say, "There
> just ain't no liquor but Jeppson for me today!"

George built an entire campaign around "Quitchyerbellyachin'" and the idea of starting hours of drinking with a shot of Malört. It was a message for the moment. Just twenty years removed from Prohibition, the nation was in the middle of a decades-long boozy boom, an era of heavy drinking and heavily masculine drinking: three-martini lunches for the white collar and hours in neighborhood bars for the blue. Drinking was a national pastime; drinking deep into the night was ritual. Beer was king, but spirits began a twenty-year climb that saw them briefly grow just as popular, a national swilling of liquors clear, brown, or mixed into bright, glowing cocktails.

George took his message beyond newspaper ads, to the places he was sure to find his audience: Chicago's neighborhood bars. He distributed "Quitchyerbellyachin'" cocktail napkins and white table tents, offered free to tavern owners, featuring an X-ray of a skull. Below, it read:

MY WIFE HAD MY HEAD EXAMINED!
Going round and round was,

"Quitchyerbellyachin',
I Start My Drinking With
Jeppson!"
WHY DON'T YOU?

———————

Talking to drinkers was crucial, but George used the dialogue to court an even more important audience: the people between him and the drinkers.

He sent frequent updates to store and bar owners, sometimes on letterhead ("Personally from George Brode") or as a newsletter he called *Jeppson Jots* ("Jottings and news of interest about Jeppson's Malört"), touting his product at the intersection of humor and masculinity with a dash of pop psychology. George knew his drinkers didn't live in the leafy suburbs or in twenty-fourth-floor lakefront condominiums; they were, he told bar owners in one mailing, "men of independence."

They worked with their hands through the sweat and heat of Chicago's stockyards, slaughtering millions of animals across three shifts a day to feed the nation, or in the acrid steel plants of southeastern Chicago and Northwest Indiana. Their neighborhoods, shrouded in smoke and dust from the mills, were anchored in the taverns. A half-mile stretch could pack in a dozen or more, functioning as both social lifeblood and air-conditioned oases, heavily male arenas packed with everymen. At least that's how George saw his audience.

"We don't believe Jeppson drinkers, present and potential, are so sophisticated that they overlook the human, ordinary every day facts of living," George wrote in one letter to bar owners. Drinkers must therefore be spoken to in their own language, he said. Jeppson's Malört was their language.

George tried enlisting bar owners and shopkeepers as his partners and salespeople, offering free blown-up copies of his "lots and lots of advertisements in Chicagoland newspapers," more commonly taken out in Chicago's liberal, working-class newspaper, the *Sun-Times*, than in the more conservative *Tribune*.

"You . . . as the enterprisingly successful retailer . . . should avail yourself of Jeppson reprints and blow-ups," he wrote. "Can't you just see your customer stepping up to your bar or counter—being reminded to ask for Jeppson—so you can make the easy sale?"

He included a hand-drawn image of a bald man with oversized eyes and ears with an elongated tongue, on which was written JEPPSON. He asked tavern owners to hang it behind their bars.

> This campaign of humor and laughter is no odd occurrence. Our Jeppson drinker—the horny-handed male artisan—is in the nature of a movement. We ask you to confirm our belief that the growing number of Jeppson male drinkers reflects an enormous effort by the individual through the means of his drink preference to escape and resist conformity. The result is something ex-ci-ting . . . a person in his very male-ness is claiming recognition.
>
> How you, the seller/server of Jeppson can help: In order to talk effectively to today's drinker of hard liquor . . . you must reach him at his own personal level. You bridge the gap between yourself and the prospective customer by that one, never failing instrument in communications—what we're talking about is humor, the quip, the hearty joke, the cartoon, or the smile. THIS . . . the enclosed Jeppson "hang up" cards are designed to do for you!

And then there were the distribution companies.

In a bid to regulate alcohol sales after the end of Prohibition, the nation adopted a three-tiered system to regulate how booze—whether beer, wine, or spirits—moved through the market. The goal was a buffer between the manufacturer (in this case, George) and retailer (whether a bar or store). Sandwiched between was the second tier, generally out of sight to drinkers but an engine of the system.

Often operated as small, family-owned companies, each with a unique territory canvassed by a team of middle-class salesmen, distributors bought alcohol from manufacturers and sold it at a markup to shops, bars,

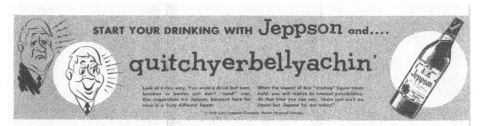

The first of a 1957 Series of Advertisements
that is appearing in your
Daily Newspapers

George stayed in close contact with distributors, often touting his advertising efforts behind Jeppson's Malört. *Courtesy of Pat Gabelick*

stadiums, and restaurants across the city. Liquor and beer distribution would consolidate in the decades to come, but in the 1950s and '60s, George worked with dozens of them—as many as forty at a time—to sell Jeppson's Malört across Chicago. On yellow legal paper stapled into a green ledger, he tracked sales: distributor by distributor, month by month, year by year.

He addressed their monthly sales meetings, giving the salesmen fresh zeal for nudging proprietors toward his brand. Distributors had hundreds of products to manage; George couldn't assume they would prioritize Malört. He needed to *make* them prioritize Malört.

Just as George stayed in touch with bar owners, he was in frequent contact with his distributors, sending copies of his newspaper advertisements with rah-rah enthusiasm: "Greatest liquor campaign ever . . . this message will appear in your daily newspapers, on windows, backbars, counters, and billboards." He kept a list of distributor salesmen and their home addresses to send updates directly. He wrote each letter by hand, had his secretary type it, made edits, then had her type it again. On it would go until George was satisfied.

He offered incentives as absurd as his product. Krazy Klox kept time running backward. Ordering two cases of Jeppson's Malört—twenty-four bottles—got a bar owner one Krazy Klok. Five cases earned three

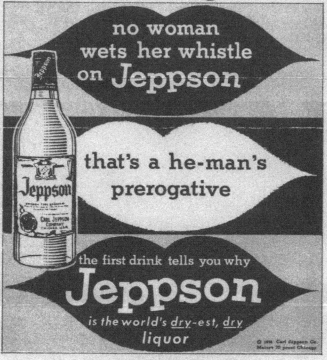

George often leaned into the masculinity of drinking Jeppson's Malört, both in advertising and when appealing to his distributors. *Courtesy of Pat Gabelick*

Krazy Klox. Even more successful was a tie giveaway. Distribution salesmen were sent random colors based on how many new customers they secured; they'd inevitably call the office to ask for specific colors to round out their collections. By the mid-1960s, when those calls came in, packing up the ties and sending them off fell to George's young secretary, Pat.

Just as she thought George's ads were silly, she found the communications with bartenders and distributors corny and, frankly, sort of dumb. Then again, she never tasted Malört, and she wasn't interested. She knew she wasn't the audience.

After the demise of Red Horse Liquors, George shifted production of Jeppson's Malört two and a half miles northwest, to Mar-Salle Chicago, a former rival sitting a block from a fork in the Chicago River.

Like Red Horse and Bielzoff Products before it, Mar-Salle was a family business, pumping out hundreds of brands—gins, vodkas, brandies, and sugary flavored liqueurs. In an era before industry consolidation, before the rise of global conglomerates, small liquor companies could compete in bars and stores well enough to pass through the generations.

Harry Jacobi started Mar-Salle in December 1933, as soon as Prohibition ended. Nineteen years later he handed the company to his son, Jack, and daughter, Muriel; they steered the business through the next thirty years. Both siblings had sons who also joined the business: Muriel's son, Chris Mitchell, worked summers at Mar-Salle as a high school student in the 1960s. Jack's son, Greg Jacobi, started as a high school sophomore in the early 1970s.

Among Chris Mitchell's first jobs at the family business was chopping three-foot stalks of wormwood into three-inch pieces to push into each bottle of Jeppson's Malört before filling. It was one of George's marketing ideas. Fifteen-year-old Chris sneaked his first taste of Malört about then. He thought it must be like drinking dandelions.

Greg Jacobi started at Mar-Salle a few years later, and he, too, helped make Malört, first by bottling it and later, as the head of production after college, by climbing on a forklift to dump huge boxes of wormwood into one-thousand-gallon steel tanks before the alcohol flooded in. Greg never much liked drinking Malört, but he had the rare ability to taste it without flinching. In his early twenties, he always brought a bottle to parties, challenging any big talker to take a shot while keeping a straight face. No one could ever pull it off. The stunt was an inevitable hit.

Mar-Salle sent more than five hundred thousand gallons of spirits into the market each year and owned nearly all the brands it produced. Jeppson's Malört was a rare outlier. George had it made in small quantities, about 420 cases at a time, seven or eight times a year, depending on the flow of business.

It was just a wisp of a brand on Mar-Salle's production schedule, but the deal worked for both sides. George got his Malört, and the Jacobi family got a little extra business from someone they enjoyed working with. George was a conscientious client—thoughtful, gentlemanly, and always prompt to pay his bills. The Jacobi family admired him and his odd project; it seemed as if George wrung as much business from Malört as anyone possibly could.

George came by Mar-Salle often in a decades-long relationship, always the finest-dressed person from the moment he arrived—a crisp suit in a sea of denim. He tasted every new batch of Malört before it shipped from the warehouse, swishing it in his mouth until confident it was properly off-putting. Then he spit it out.

By the mid-1960s, George was all in on the zaniness, and the growing lore of Jeppson's Malört. He pivoted from "Quitchyerbellyachin'" to a new campaign upping Malört's brashness: "Are you man enough to drink Jeppson?"

The posters came in striking colors, each conveying a single sentiment reflecting a chest-thumping 1960s-era masculinity: "When baby blue is your favorite color—don't drink Jeppson" (accompanied by a cartoon image of a preening man); "Do you wear a beret because it becomes you? Don't drink Jeppson" (the same preening man wearing a red beret); "If

Malört ads from 1963.
Courtesy of Pat Gabelick

your only exercise is to curl your mustache—don't dare drink Jeppson" (accompanied by an image of a man twirling his mustache). Each was punctuated with the tagline "It's a real man's drink!"

George upped his marketing, investing in olive-green tags dangling from the neck of each bottle, taunting prospective drinkers: "Are you man enough to drink our two-fisted liquor?"

Inside were ten cocktail recipes rooted in George's imagination— Malört mixed with Scotch or gin or vodka or a variety of juices—plus a two-page ode to Malört with curious capitalization and rife with exaggeration, if not outright falsehood:

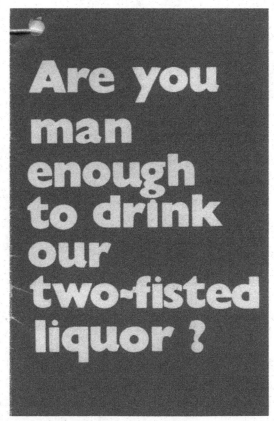

For close to forty years, booklets hung around the necks of Jeppson's Malört bottles taunting prospective drinkers, asking whether they were "man enough" to drink the bitter spirit within. *Courtesy of Pat Gabelick*

THE STORY OF JEPPSON MALORT

jeppson malort is one liquor derived wholly from maceration and extraction of a singularly wild-growing plant, hand gathered from certain northern European mountainsides. The painstaking method used in arriving at its basic taste, found only in jeppson malort, has not changed in centuries of application. Rarely do climatic conditions of wind, rain, sun and soil combine in successive years in these botanicals to yield the desired taste. Experience shows that only one gathering in four years is capable of producing the unique flavor, taste and color of jeppson malort.

JEPPSON MALORT DIFFERS
FROM OTHER LIQUORS

Let's face it, most first-time drinkers of jeppson malort are repelled by our liquor. Its strong taste is definitely not for everyone. This liquor is so rough and ready, so rugged, unrelenting (and even brutal) to the taste that the last fifty-five years of sales in America shows only 1 out of 49 men (rarely women) continue drinking jeppson malort beyond the first "shock-glass".

During Carl Jeppson's lifetime he was apt to say, "We're not fooling ourselves, we know we can't take drinkers away from bourbon and rye blends, gin or vodka. jeppson malort is made for that small percentage of Americans who don't favor light, neutered spirits."

IT TAKES QUITE A MAN TO
DRINK JEPPSON MALORT

Once you drink our two-fisted liquor, you'll never forget it. Persist and you'll find a gratifying unique flavor. As a "regular" jeppson malort drinker you have latched on to one liquor whose taste lingers and lasts, seemingly forever.

JEPPSON MALORT
drinks

"SHOCK-GLASS" ©
1½ oz. jeppson malort in a shot glass.
Down the hatch in one swallow.

JEPPSONI (dry-est martini)
One-half part jeppson malort
4 parts: 90 proof gin or 100 proof vodka
Stir with cracked ice; strain into cocktail
glasses. Serve with olives or lemon peel
twists.

VIKING
Pour 2 oz. jeppson malort over ice cubes
in a highball glass. Add club soda to fill.
Stir gently.

SWEET SWEDE ©
(ancient mariner recipe)
Drink jeppson malort straight after
placing a sugar cube in mouth.

JEPPSON MALORT
drinks

NORDIC PERIL
1½ oz. jeppson malort
3 oz. grapefruit juice
In a short glass filled with ice. Stir.
Garnish with thin slice of lime.

J M & V
Pour one part jeppson malort and one
part vodka (preferably 100 proof) over
ice cubes in old fashioned glass.
Garnish with available roughage.

JEPPSON MANHATTAN
½ oz. jeppson malort
1½ oz. bourbon or rye whiskey
Stir with cracked ice and strain into
glass. Add a cherry.

JEPPSON COLLINS
1½ oz. jeppson malort
1 oz. grapefruit juice
1 teaspoon sugar
In tall glass dissolve sugar in juice; add
jeppson malort and ice cubes; fill with 7-
Up or Squirt.

JEPPSON MALORT
drinks

SUISSE
Pour 4 oz. jeppson malort into a suisse
glass.
　　(Especially made to allow shaved ice to
　　melt slowly and drip into center cup
　　containing liquor.)
Pack outer glass shell with shaved ice. Sip
through two short straws.

ROB ROY
½ oz. jeppson malort
1½ oz. Scotch
Stir with cracked ice and strain into cocktail
glass. Add twist of lemon peel.

OUTRIGGER
1½ oz. jeppson malort
Juice of ½ lime
Pineapple juice
Fill tall glass with crushed ice. Add lime juice,
jeppson malort. Fill with pineapple juice. Stir.

JEPPSON MALORT

the
two fisted
liquor

Two-Fisted Liquor is a copyright of the Carl Jeppson
Company, Chicago, USA. 35% alc./vol.
© 1990

The booklets included an array of basic cocktail recipes from George's imagination, part of his endless effort to make a challenging spirit more appealing.
Courtesy of Pat Gabelick

For all his efforts to sell Jeppson's Malört, George was already at peace with a hard truth: those efforts would likely never pay off.

Most years he sold two thousand to three thousand cases—barely enough for Malört to justify its own existence. George's zest for marketing only made the operation more expensive, and returns rarely repaid the investment. "Newspaper campaign 'a waste,'" he scribbled to himself while tabulating annual sales one winter. Without his law practice and personal finances, Jeppson's Malört wouldn't have stood a chance.

Coming out of Prohibition a generation earlier, most liquor brands were modest performers dependent on regional appeal. In the decades that followed, giants were born. Jack Daniel's Tennessee Whiskey surged after the war, so much so that for twenty years, bars and stores could only get the small amounts they were given. Jack Daniel's built advertising campaigns around demand outstripping supply, which only pushed it deeper into the culture: two hundred thousand cases sold annually in the 1950s became tens of millions sold in the decades to come.

Jeppson's Malört had no such good fortune. There was always as much Malört as anyone needed. More, in fact. Much more.

In reality George was lucky to find any audience. Just as he bought Malört, Chicago's Swedish population shifted from immigrants and their first-generation children to the second and third generations, which assimilated into the middle class and fled for the suburbs. They had no attachment to the intensely bitter spirit their parents and grandparents drank.

Replacing them in the neighborhoods was a new wave of immigrants, including hundreds of thousands of Poles following World War II. Many of the arrivals were delighted to find Jeppson's Malört at the corner bars; it tasted just like *piołunówka*, a bitter Polish digestif made with wormwood nearly impossible to find outside their home country. Malört was an entirely suitable replacement.

Then came another new audience: native Spanish speakers. As Mexicans, Puerto Ricans, and Central Americans became the backbone of working-class Chicago, they filled the neighborhood bars once occupied by Swedes and other European immigrants. Like the Poles, they adopted Malört as their own—so much so that by the 1960s, George began advertising in Chicago's Spanish-language daily newspapers.

It was all just enough to keep Malört afloat. And by the mid-1960s, George's efforts finally, albeit modestly, paid off: for the next decade, he sold more than 3,000 cases per year. Sales peaked in 1973, when George sold 3,846 cases of Jeppson's Malört—the most he would ever sell during his lifetime.

4

PAT AND GEORGE

No one was closer to George than Pat.

It was at first easy to explain. It was just the two of them, alone five days a week in that fourteenth-floor office, Pat as George's gatekeeper: answerer of his phone, opener of his mail, keeper of his calendar.

When Fritzi needed money, she didn't ask George. She called Pat. George put Fritzi on an allowance, and when she exceeded it—often, thanks to betting on mah-jongg most afternoons with friends—she was more likely to get a check by appealing to her husband's secretary than to her husband. Pat always advocated for her.

But Pat's relationship with George quietly changed. In January 1967, after not quite a year of working for him, George asked her to join him on a business trip downstate. He said he needed her to take notes. Pat was surprised at the invitation and wondered if she should read more into it. Their relationship changed on that trip. He was fifty-seven. She was twenty-three.

Pat didn't think much of it, in part because it was familiar terrain. The job at Automatic Canteen hadn't worked out because of an affair with a man ten years older, a married father of five. Pat saw him across the room while sitting at her desk and knew she wanted him. She had him, and soon he was promising they'd run off to Florida together. Pat gave her cat away in preparation for what she believed would be a move south.

The man's wife found out—Pat never learned how—and asked to

meet in a bar near her home. Pat agreed, numbing herself with whiskey for what she thought would be a hard conversation about starting a new life with the woman's husband. Instead, the woman said her husband was going nowhere. He'd cheated before and he'd cheat again. In the meantime, she said, Pat's relationship with him was over.

Pat got drunk and called her mother and said she didn't want to live anymore. Pat's mother called the police, who tracked Pat down and got her safely home. Next, her mother called Automatic Canteen. Both Pat and the man were fired. Weeks later she went to work for George. (She also got her cat back.)

Once her relationship with George changed during their trip downstate, it changed again two weeks later when Chicago's legendary blizzard of 1967 paralyzed the city with nearly two feet of snow. Pat and George spent two nights downtown during the storm—one at the Bismarck Hotel, two blocks from the office, and because that room was too small for Pat's liking, the next night at the Sherman House, another block on. He stayed as long as he could, until he had to go home.

Pat still didn't think much of it. Even as she began calling him "George" instead of "Mr. Brode," she kept dating men her own age. George's jealousy was palpable, but he had no justification for it. Pat saw it and appreciated it. They spent more time together.

Pat offered George a world his wife didn't. Fritzi was warm and gregarious and happiest in her own social orbit, kibitzing with friends and playing cards late into the night. Cards were the center of her weekend socializing with George—he played gin rummy with the men; she chatted over mah-jongg with the women—even if he would have preferred a night at the symphony. Fritzi's ideal vacation was a trip to Las Vegas or a cruise with friends. George didn't care much for Vegas, cruises, or traveling with friends. He grudgingly did them all but would rather have been alone with his wife in the south of France.

Pat was glad to do whatever George wanted. She had little exposure to the grandeur of downtown Chicago—the museums, the restaurants, the theaters—while growing up in her working-class suburb just a few miles away. She'd never even tasted wine. George was eager to share those things with Pat. She was thrilled to experience them.

They subscribed to a series of weekend theater matinees, usually preceded by lunch in the tiki-style splendor of Trader Vic's, the Polynesian chain housed in the basement of the Palmer House hotel. Pat would pick at crab Rangoon and sip Singapore slings surrounded by the illusion of beachfront thatched huts on a Saturday afternoon—sheer extravagance for a working-class suburban girl. Sometimes after the performance, instead of bothering with a hotel, they went back to the office.

George wasn't the sort to shower Pat with gifts or money, but he was attentive and kind in a way he wasn't with his wife or sons. And just as Pat was agreeable to whatever he wanted to do, he was open to whatever Pat suggested. They picnicked a hundred miles southwest of the city, on the cliffs above Starved Rock State Park. They saw Johnny Cash at the Wisconsin State Fair in 1969. George barely knew who Johnny Cash was but had a wonderful time.

A year into their relationship, George sent Pat to a seminar for legal secretaries in New York City, then flew out to meet her. They saw three shows in three nights—*Hair, George M!,* and jazzy pop duo Steve and Eydie—and dined at the Rainbow Room. Pat had heard of the Plaza, the famed hotel at the foot of Central Park, and wanted to stay there. George got them a room at the Plaza.

George told Fritzi he was in New York for work.

At dinner one night in downtown Chicago, they ran into David and his girlfriend. They played it off as dinner between boss and secretary after a long workday. It seemed plausible. Fritzi was off playing cards with friends. What else was George supposed to do?

They were less fortunate when stopping for lunch at a crepes restaurant on a Saturday afternoon before the Gold Coast Art Fair, an annual summer highlight for well-heeled Chicago couples. Pat looked over at the next table and her stomach dropped: sitting there was a group of Fritzi's friends. Pat panicked and swelled with embarrassment. By the end of the day, Fritzi surely would know.

George didn't seem concerned. It wasn't his way. He was also at peace with a simple truth: at some point, he knew Fritzi knew. Pat also came to realize Fritzi knew. She and Fritzi never talked about it, and Pat learned not to fret. If anything, she had the upper hand. She was younger, she spent more time with George, and she never doubted he preferred her company. Fritzi wasn't happy with the situation and confided as much to her sister. She was ultimately resigned to it, comfortable in her life and content to avoid an ugly divorce that could leave her with nothing.

Pat wasn't always happy with the situation either. Sometimes it bothered her that George had his life and she had hers, and the intersection of the two only happened at work or on weekends while George lied to his wife. The relationship mostly worked for her, though. She never asked him to leave Fritzi. She knew he wouldn't.

For decades, Pat wondered what drew her to a man thirty-four years older.

Some of the answer was what binds any two people. George was kind to her. He was understanding. There was tenderness between them. Pat never recoiled from a fight, especially after a few drinks. She had a temper and could throw things in a rage, and she did it more than once, hurling stacks of files against the wall for reasons she wouldn't even remember. She drank far more than George—Canadian whiskey on the rocks with a twist when she was young, wine as she got older, sometimes several glasses in an evening—yet he never judged her. She was thin when they met and struggled with her weight over the years. He never said a word. He was patient with her, certainly more than with his wife. Pat heard him raise his voice to Fritzi many times on the phone. He never did it to Pat. A younger man, Pat thought, wouldn't have the ability to navigate her.

She was engaged once, when she was nineteen, to a man ten years older. They met in a bar where Pat was a regular, introduced by the bar's owner. Pat's mother and grandmother loved the guy. He talked of moving to a small town and raising kids. Pat returned the ring after two weeks, figuring she was too young, destined to wind up divorced or a cheating wife. She never regretted the decision. She dated other men, but nothing serious. George became one of the steadiest relationships of her life—romantic or otherwise.

Pat's mother was always there. Her father, John, a welder, was a phantom. He contracted tuberculosis when Pat was a baby and moved out of the house to recover in a sanatorium on Chicago's North Side. Pat and her mother visited occasionally, though Pat could never go inside; she waved to him through a window. She'd mostly remember the visits for chasing rabbits across the lawn.

Pat's grandparents moved into the house while her father was gone, and to a child who didn't know any difference, it felt like the way things should be. She grew tight with her grandfather; he took her sledding and to the circus and became the nurturing father figure she never knew. After two years, John Gabelick moved back in and her grandparents left. Three-year-old Pat was crushed.

When Pat was ten, her mother was diagnosed with breast cancer. Radiation left her in pain and struggling to breathe for the rest of her life. Pat's parents separated a few years later, and her father left town, first to Duluth, then to Omaha.

Pat saw her father only once more. She took an overnight train to Omaha after graduation and met some of his friends and his new girlfriend, Bonnie. It was a good visit, and Pat started to think she and her father might forge the relationship they never had as she grew up.

It wasn't to be. A few nights in, while walking through the courtyard of his apartment building, she heard footsteps from behind, then felt a blow to her head. Pat fell to the ground and lay there, screaming and screaming. Whatever the attacker was after, he didn't get; as she screamed, he ran. Pat went to the hospital for stitches, then went home early.

Months later a letter arrived. Pat's father said she wouldn't hear from him for a long time. He'd never divorced Pat's mother and still sent her money. He wanted to marry Bonnie and to move on. So he disappeared.

Pat tracked him down twenty years later through the Social Security Administration. They exchanged a few letters, and Pat learned he moved to Kansas City and then to Henderson, Nevada. He and Bonnie had a son and a daughter—two half siblings Pat never knew existed.

Pat thought she might see him again, but on the way home from his son's wedding, passing through a record snowstorm in the mountains near Lake Tahoe, John Gabelick's car slid off the road. He died months later in the hospital at the age of seventy-five.

As the years went by, Pat wondered if George fulfilled a father complex for her.

———————

Everything shifted in 1977. Fritzi died that May, at the age of sixty-five. She was in the hospital for cancer treatment and seemed to be doing OK when she had a fatal heart attack. George was shocked more than anything. He was sad but not devastated.

That fall Pat's mother, Genevieve, also died. She was fifty-seven. Her cancer had returned, and care fell to Pat—up at dawn to drive her mother to the hospital, back home to make coffee and breakfast, then back to the city for a day of work with George. Genevieve had cared for Pat's grandmother; now that job also fell to Pat. Months later Pat's grandmother died too.

For ten years Pat and George built a relationship within a set of walls: his marriage, her ailing mother and grandmother, their work. In less than a year, the walls fell away.

Things became easier. More relaxed. Almost as soon as Fritzi died, Pat and George spent Sundays, in addition to Saturdays, together—the opera, the symphony, afternoon piano concerts. They traveled more. George spent nights at Pat's house in the suburbs.

They kept things quiet for a while. George's friends knew Pat only as his secretary, and even with Fritzi gone, there was no easy way to reveal she was more than that. After a couple years, Pat said enough. She told George she wanted to be part of his life.

They tried going out with his friends, which was awkward at first but became easier. They tried going out with her friends; that was harder. Pat could more easily bridge the age gap up than George could bridge it down. Pat grew close to some of the wives of George's friends, often in a mother-daughter dynamic.

After a few years, Pat was ready to get married. George resisted. Pat vented about it to her therapist, and the therapist asked George to sit in on a session. He grudgingly did and said he just didn't want to be married again. Simple as that. Pat broke up with him and said she wouldn't work for him either.

She went back after two days. She knew she wouldn't follow through. She also knew George well enough to know he was sincere. He'd been married once. He was done.

Pat thought she deserved financial and emotional security after a decade of sneaking around, but she made peace with his decision. As they drove past the handsome stone chapel on the Northwestern University campus, Pat couldn't resist needling George: "That's where I want to get married!" she cooed. George would grow defensive. Pat smiled every time.

There was no grand reveal to George's kids. At some point they all just knew, and the truth was they had known for years. Pat joined George for Thanksgiving at his daughter Judy's house in Glencoe. Judy was only ever gracious to Pat.

Pat and George settled into their days together. She would ask about life before her, about his childhood in immigrant-filled Humboldt Park, the subjects he studied and the games he played. He was never interested in the discussion. Either he didn't remember or he didn't want to

George and Pat in Bath, England, in the late 1980s. Travel was core to their relationship. *Courtesy of Pat Gabelick*

remember. He was instead a selective storyteller, quick to tout graduating from Northwestern but never, in all the years he and Pat were together, mentioning two years at a junior college.

George was more interested in relishing the present. They visited his cousins in Los Angeles and drove up the coast; San Francisco became Pat's favorite city. When George fished along the Mississippi River in Wisconsin, Pat tagged along, reading books in the lodge while he was on the water. They traveled to theater festivals in Canada and museums in Washington, DC. They went to New York City a couple times a year, George always making a point of bringing corned beef sandwiches from Carnegie Deli back to the room, often as a midnight snack. They flew to London. Italy. Germany for Christmas. Yellowstone and the Tetons. A car trip through Arizona. Pat had never seen the desert, and it did nothing for her, but she loved Sedona. As soon as they turned off the highway toward its fabled red rocks, she knew it was for her. They spent a Christmas there, in a cabin along a creek. It snowed. It was magical.

They flew to Florida, where Pat insisted they visit Disney World. She loved Disney World. George didn't care for it, but he wanted Pat to be happy. So he went. The real reason for that trip, though, was to make Jeppson's Malört.

5

JUST BE PATIENT

JEPPSON'S MALÖRT LIVED three lives across its first sixty years: from Carl Jeppson's homespun attempt to appeal to fellow Swedish immigrants to George Broide's acquisition as a young liquor company executive to thirty-three years of production at Mar-Salle as George Brode's unlikely middle-aged side project.

In 1986 Jeppson's Malört entered its fourth life. For the first time, Chicago's odd and bitter liqueur would not be made in Chicago.

The shift was spurred by a calculation Jack Jacobi made in the late 1970s, after nearly thirty years in the liquor business. Mar-Salle supported two generations of the Jacobi family, but industry consolidation was in its earliest days. Conglomerates grew larger. Jack needed to either grow the business or get out.

He got out. In 1980 he sold Mar-Salle to Abe Schecter, a Chicago businessman doing the opposite of the Jacobi family—he was looking to grow. Two years earlier, Schecter bought Medley Distilling in Owensboro, Kentucky, just across the border from Indiana, along a bend in the Ohio River. Medley was a midsize operation capitalizing on the mid-century whiskey boom; its flagship brand, Ezra Brooks bourbon, was a Jack Daniel's knockoff introduced in the late 1950s.

Schecter bought Mar-Salle with plans to shift production from Chicago to Owensboro, but only after a few years, to ease the transition. In 1986 he finally migrated its dozens of brands to Kentucky. Zarnov

Vodka. Valley Gold Rum. Hawaiian Blu Curacao. Mar-Salle Brandy. And Jeppson's Malört.

Malört production didn't last long in Kentucky. Only two batches, in late 1987, were made there. Schecter sold Medley to the larger Glenmore Distillery, which moved production yet again, to its more modern facility just a few miles away—but declined to take Jeppson's Malört along.

Between the meager volumes, handling the wormwood, and the neck-dangling booklets that hung from every bottle, it was simply too much work for too little payoff. George pleaded with Glenmore to keep him as a client. They refused. Jeppson's Malört was without a home. In 1988 not a drop was made.

It would have been an easy moment to give up, to call it a good run for a strange product with diminishing returns. The thirty-five hundred cases George sold each year in the mid-1960s and mid-1970s—no juggernaut, but respectable—fell by nearly a third in the mid-1980s. He was stuck at twenty-five hundred cases and hadn't crossed the three-thousand-case threshold since 1974.

George was seventy-nine years old and had plenty of money. Retirement was an obvious option. But he felt vital as ever. He still traveled with Pat, so much so that she could feel like a cruise director as George awaited news of their next adventure. He still walked the four miles home from work each afternoon. He was still consumed with Jeppson's Malört.

As he'd done for decades, George stayed in close touch with his distributors, addressing their sales meetings and checking in throughout the year. He called the biggest distributors every couple months and prodded the smallest too, strategizing to boost sales. In 1987 he proposed a five-dollar bonus for each new Jeppson's Malört placement at a suburban distributor that sold a meager twenty-five cases the year before. The incentive didn't help much. The next year it only sold thirty-six.

The truth was that George's little brand sold barely one-tenth of one percent of the most popular vodkas, and his sales were falling. Yet he remained enthralled, not with the drink itself, which he found as off-putting as most other people, but with the hobby, the dabbling, the challenge—all were uniquely his. They had been his for more than fifty years. Jeppson's Malört outlasted his career in the liquor industry,

Of the dozens of brands David managed through twenty years at Florida Distillers, Malört became his favorite—the odd, lovable misfit child. He could barely fathom it existed, let alone that it was his responsibility to make it.

When a friend headed to Chicago, whether for vacation or business, he said to look for a bottle of Jeppson's Malört at whatever bar they wandered into. If it wasn't there, he said, it wasn't a bar worth visiting.

The reality was that fewer and fewer bars were carrying Malört. Times and tastes had changed.

The old-timers who drank it were either dying off or moving to the Sunbelt. Chicago's neighborhood bars were disappearing, a decline rooted in the law-and-order promises of Mayor Richard J. Daley, first elected in 1955. Daley saw taverns as nests of violence, drugs, and prostitution; during his twenty-one-year reign, his administration revoked hundreds of liquor licenses. By the late 1980s, Chicago was home to about half as many taverns as in the 1940s. Those taverns were the lifeblood for Jeppson's Malört. If the bitter yellow-green shot wasn't going to be downed in neighborhood bars, where would it be downed?

A broader cultural shift also unfolded as Chicago transformed from blue-collar bulwark to white-collar economic engine. The stockyards closed in 1971. The South Side steel plants soon followed. Between the late 1970s and late 1980s, tens of thousands of middle-class union jobs disappeared—and with them, countless Jeppson's Malört drinkers.

Meanwhile, the bill came due on the boozy excesses of the previous thirty years. Alcoholism was finally considered a disease, drunk driving was acknowledged as a public scourge, and the idea of "recovery" was entrenched in the public consciousness, with more than a million participants in Alcoholics Anonymous. By the end of the '80s, over the furious objection of the industry, warnings of potential health problems and birth defects adorned every bottle or can of wine, beer, and spirits in America.

Bourbon sales cratered amid a thirty-year dip. The beer industry atrophied into a shrinking number of conglomerates. Ronald Reagan's

America wanted safe, predictable flavors: the blandness of Bud Light and Bartles & Jaymes—not the brawn of brown liquor, and certainly not the bracing bitterness of a strange yellow-green one.

A dwindling number of Chicago bars kept Malört around, whether as a habit or a means to drive off pests and interlopers. When a customer asked for a free shot at P.O.E.T.S., a blue-collar bar hanging on along fabled Division Street, the owner offered a mixture of ginger schnapps and Jeppson's Malört—the worst combination he could think of. No customer ever asked for a free shot again. Through his advertising and marketing, George Brode spent years laughing with Malört. Now the world laughed mostly at it. Year after year, Carl Jeppson Co. lost money. Some declines were meager ($727 in 1981) and others more meaningful ($16,575 in 1979).

Through the 1980s, Malört held on mostly as a relic and an oddity. In pastoral southwestern Wisconsin, the Malört Society formed in 1984, started by Michael Riddet, a wildlife artist who discovered Malört as a twenty-one-year-old bartender in suburban Chicago in the late '70s. He was brainstorming fundraisers to save the old hotel in downtown Boscobel, Wisconsin, when he stumbled on the idea of a club whose means of entry was a shot of Malört from a dirty ashtray. Riddet soon agreed to allow clean ashtrays for initiation, which allowed the society to eventually count more than six hundred members. They even made lapel pins.

Months after forming the club, Riddet sent George a letter, alerting him to his fans north of the border and lamenting that Malört was not available beyond Chicago; Riddet stocked up when visiting Chicago or when friends visited him. George responded promptly, projecting the image of an operation far larger than Carl Jeppson Co. was:

> February 20, 1985
> Dear Mr. Riddet,
> I enjoyed your letter immensely. Despite limitations on the production of Jeppson Malort, due to inadequate supply of our singular wild-growing botanical hand gathered on

certain European mountain sides, I shall inquire of our sales
staff to seek a Wisconsin wholesale liquor dealer who would
be interested in supplying the bars in Boscobel.

You could help by asking the owners of the restaurant
and the bar to furnish the name of your wholesalers who
we can contact.

Once a source and supply of Jeppson Malort has been
established, you can count on the support of our marketing
people to further the aims of your Malort Society.
Cordially,
George Brode

In Chicago, Malört survived mostly at the bars catering to old-timers
and the working class, or at the fleeting few still rooted in Swedish heritage, places like Simon's Tavern. With a Swedish flag out front, Simon's
was one of the old-guard bars in Andersonville, a historically Swedish
neighborhood turning less Swedish by the year. Few people were more
passionate about Malört than Simon's owner Scott Martin, whose Swedish
family used it as a cure for stomachaches when he was a boy. His first
taste came at the age of eight.

When Martin bought Simon's, he was the rare barkeep to know
exactly what Malört was, and at an old-school Swedish bar, he relentlessly
touted its merits, waving the booklet dangling from its neck—"Are you
man enough to drink our two-fisted liquor?"—to taunt customers into a
shot. Simon's became one of the best Malört accounts in the city, selling
enough to elicit a phone call one afternoon as Martin tended bar.

"What are you guys doing there?" a gravelly voice said on the other
end of the line.

"What?" Martin said.

"I said what are you guys doing there!"

"Who's calling?"

"This is George Brode."

"The guy from Malört?!"

"Yeah—what are you doing? No one sells two cases of Malört a
month anymore!"

Martin explained his history with the brand. George thanked him for being a good customer.

George relished the small victories and soldiered on. An unsolicited order was cause for celebration. So was a distributor somehow managing to sell as many cases as it had the year before. Into his eighties, George tracked sales as doggedly as he had thirty years earlier, with notes that cheered every win and lamented every retreat:

> 10/03/85—Rappin ordered 200 cases. On hand: a <u>mere</u> 2 cases.
>
> 1/23/86—Spoke with Larry Marszalek. Has 37 cases on hand—had called last Monday, no answer. At my insistence placed 250 case order for 2/03 pickup! Depletion equal to 20 cases a week!!!
>
> 8/03/87—Bill Locke deferred ordering until next month. Reports on hand 51 cases. Depletion since May 1 for 3 months (92 days) is .9022/day, a significant decline from 1.17/day prior period.
>
> 10/08/91—Spoke with Joe Costello about slow sales. He said every item they have is down. Nothing is moving. Even if you dropped your price $20 it wouldn't help. Just be patient, he said.

Patience only went so far. In the early 1990s, Jeppson's Malört case sales slid under two thousand for the first time in fifty years. They'd poke back up for a year as George doubled down on sales or marketing, then drop to a new low.

By 1992 sales had fallen to 1,541 cases—down sixty percent from the peak less than twenty years earlier. Once selling Malört to dozens of distributors across Chicago, George was left with two. Consolidation shrunk the industry, and the years shrunk the appetite for Malört.

Despite the long decline, George remained an optimist. His sales notes, once stretching pages, included just one observation in 1997, when he was eighty-six years old and in his last full year of operating Jeppson's Malört:

Judge & Dolph <u>sold</u> 220-1/2 cases (highest ever) in June, running out of inventory!

George would never know it, but one day his optimism would prove well founded.

6

THEY FOUND IT IN
EACH OTHER

GEORGE BRODE DIED on a warm, cloudy Thursday evening in August 1999, and it appeared his beloved Jeppson's Malört was dying with him.

Sales were stuck below two thousand cases per year, and the marketing efforts, once one of his great joys, stopped. The year George died, sales skidded to the lowest total of his sixty-five years with the brand: a scant 1,163 cases. Nearly thirty years earlier, the figure was almost four times that.

George's last breaths came in his condominium overlooking Lake Michigan, where he had moved in 1966 with his wife, Fritzi. Now he lived there with Pat.

For thirty years, George and Pat were a couple without living under the same roof. After George resisted marrying her, Pat was content to live on her own, staying in her family's suburban home several years beyond the deaths of her mother and grandmother. She likely would have stayed in the suburbs if not for George.

By 1985, he was a vigorous seventy-six, but Pat knew there would be a time, perhaps soon, when she'd need to be closer to him. She sold the modest yellow-brick home her family had lived in for twenty-five years for just under $85,000 and moved into a twenty-sixth-floor one-bedroom apartment across the street from George. The arrangement worked for them both: weekends together and occasional dinners

during the week, but their own spaces and independence at the end
of most evenings.

They continued attending the theater and the symphony and traveled
regularly. In 1989, for his eightieth birthday, Pat surprised George with a
trip to Beverly Hills to see his cousins, Sam and Claire Franklin, whose
daughter, Bonnie, became a '70s-era television star on the sitcom *One
Day at a Time*. George didn't know where they were headed until reaching the airport. It was a wonderful surprise. George adored his cousins.

George entered his eighties gracefully, still walking the four miles
home from work most afternoons, still practicing law, and proud to
have kept Jeppson's Malört afloat after navigating the shift to Florida
Distillers. He had softened in his older age. As a younger man he was all
sharp edges and ambition. Some days he didn't even bother responding
to a polite "Good morning, Mr. Brode" from the elevator operator at the
office, leaving Pat to apologize on his behalf. For years he exaggerated

Pat and George in his Lake
Shore Drive condo in the early
1990s. *Courtesy of Pat Gabelick*

accomplishments in casual conversation. Pat cringed every time, wondering why he felt the need.

Finally, by his sixties, he relaxed, even reconciling with his son David, who in addition to starting a wealth management practice became a Broadway producer. He invited his father and Pat to New York City for one of his shows, *Into the Woods*, written by legendary playwright Stephen Sondheim. Six months later, he invited his father to join him again to attend the Tony Awards, which nominated *Into the Woods* for ten awards, including Best Musical. It lost to *The Phantom of the Opera*, but for the first time perhaps ever, the son felt acceptance and even admiration from his father.

Over dinner one night, less than a year before George died, David told Pat that his father was wholly different from when David grew up. He was softer, gentler. Pat nodded and didn't say a word, but as she saw it, George had spent more than twenty years changing—David just hadn't noticed.

———————

The beginning of the end came on a Friday morning in December 1996. Pat noticed George's gait had changed; he seemed ready to topple over at any moment. She suggested he trade in the leather dress shoes he wore for nearly seventy years for something sturdier and rubber soled.

George's vanity won out; he said he was fine. Sure enough, George slipped that Friday morning on his way to work. He was lucky to escape serious injury, but at eighty-seven years old, he could no longer put off living with Pat. He needed her. Pat moved in and ran the home: shopping, cooking, administering George's medications, and coaching him through daily rehab exercises. Eventually she helped him shower and dress.

It was a difficult transition. It wasn't that Pat didn't want to care for George; it was just hard. He was fading, slowly, and she often didn't know what to do. She found herself short on patience or wracked by nerves at the most ordinary moments, like when he walked into a public bathroom without her. What if he fell and she wasn't there? Without her, David said one night at dinner while George was in the other room, his father would almost certainly be in a nursing home. It was meant as a passing quip, maybe even with vague gratitude, but it stuck with her because it made clear that caring for George wasn't truly a choice. She had to do it.

An early Tuesday evening in November 1998 began like any other: Pat broiling lamb chops and George quietly reading the *Wall Street Journal*. Pat, needing to check the meat, used a dish towel to pull the pan from the oven. She tossed the towel back over her shoulder when she finished, unaware it had caught fire. Almost immediately there was searing pain—not even heat, just pain. She ran to a mirror and saw the unimaginable: herself on fire, flames leaping above her head.

Horrified and bewildered, she pulled her dress over her head and threw it to the ground. The fire went out quickly, but Pat writhed in pain. She had no idea how badly she was hurt. She held ice against her burns. Firefighters quickly arrived and removed the ice. They sprayed her with tepid water instead while awaiting an ambulance.

Pat underwent surgery and woke up with a tube down her throat. She panicked and started pulling it out. Doctors restrained her and filled her with sedatives for another few days as she healed. Strange, intense dreams came and went.

As she lay awake days later, she finally realized how poorly George was doing. She talked to him on the phone a couple times from the hospital, and all she wanted was concern and sympathy. She wasn't getting it. David brought George to the hospital for a visit. He barely said a word, barely made eye contact. Pat was baffled at first but then realized George couldn't do any better. Until the fire, she couldn't see it or chose not to.

Two weeks later, doctors told her there was good news: she could be home for Thanksgiving. Pat was so worn out by her recovery, and so dreaded what faced her at home, that she asked to stay a few more days. She preferred to spend Thanksgiving in the hospital.

When she was discharged, Pat finally got help caring for George. At first, it was just daytime care when she went to physical therapy. Pat handled nights. Every stray noise woke her—*Is that George?*—so she brought in a nighttime nurse over George's objections. He had the money but didn't want to spend it. Pat hired the help anyway. She slept on the couch and finally got some rest.

George kept sliding. After years of dapper dressing, he awoke one morning not knowing how to knot a tie. Pat tried to do it for him but couldn't. They were both sad and frustrated. For years he had watched the evening news to see how the stock market did that day. One night, as she prepared to make dinner, Pat asked if he was going to check his stocks.

"What stocks?" he said.

Pat took him to a neurologist. George struggled with even basic tasks like drawing clock hands at two o'clock or naming the president. He was already diagnosed with congestive heart failure. Now there was dementia.

George's body began failing. With every trip to the hospital, he seemed less likely to leave. Finally, doctors told Pat she and David needed to decide whether to let George wind down or to put him on a feeding tube that might keep him alive a few more days. David adamantly opposed the feeding tube, but it was Pat's choice, and she agonized over it for a few days. It was the last thing she thought of at night and the first thing in the morning. George was largely gone, but he occasionally perked up to say a few words. It didn't seem like much of a life, and it was far from the George she knew. She agreed to skip the feeding tube. George came home for his final days, sleeping in a hospital bed in the living room overlooking the lake as soft classical music played. Days later, he was gone.

There were flashes of regret now that Pat was alone. Hitching herself to a man thirty-four years older maybe wasn't smart planning. Well, she figured, she and George were both looking for something. They had found it in each other.

"We're talking about carving up a million or more dollars out of George's estate, and this is how I look at it," Pat Gabelick said into her attorney's answering machine early one morning in late 1999. It was five months after George died.

"I had a thirty-three-year relationship with the man," Pat continued. "I spent more than the last three years taking care of him. I was severely burned in his home making dinner for him. I'm approaching sixty with a myriad of health problems and don't feel capable of holding down a

not ready to talk about much of anything, let alone fight about money. She knew George would die before her. Still, an era of her life was over. She was fifty-six and unsure she would ever have another relationship.

She told David she just wasn't up to interviewing lawyers. So he brought them to her apartment until they found one.

That ultimately led to claims of their own. In January 2000 David asked the court for his share of George Jr.'s estimate of the value of the trusts—just over $2.1 million. Weeks later he filed a second claim, for $570,000, claiming breach of contract and "unjust enrichment," an Illinois statute applicable when "one person has received money under such circumstances that in equity and good conscience he ought not be allowed to keep it"—a reference to his brother. Finally, David filed a third claim, for $311,555, saying his father had failed to compensate him for investment advice in the late 1970s and early 1980s that ballooned $100,000 to more than $1 million.

Pat wound up getting her own lawyer, who explained that George Jr.'s suit likely wouldn't succeed; the trusts were about dodging taxes. But like David, she needed ammunition to negotiate a settlement. She filed a claim of her own, for nearly $900,000, claiming George failed to ensure she'd be financially set for the rest of her life, as he promised.

Life had devolved quickly. Five years earlier Pat was traveling with George in his last good years. Then she was caring for him as he died. Now she was recovering from devastating burns and battling his children for not only his money but also what felt like her own well-being. As long as they were together, George paid Pat a paltry salary, all of $36,000 the year he died. Friends assumed he must have paid her well as the backbone of his businesses and his romantic partner of decades. It just wasn't his way.

Pat finally realized she had been too deferential. For years George paid for everything—dinners, theater, travel—and that allowed her to live well. One day he wouldn't be there anymore, and no savings would sustain her. The day had come.

It was a strange and melancholy time. Pat became a fitful sleeper, awake most nights and typing 4:00 AM emails to pass the time. She learned George had been in prison while going through his things. Letters to Fritzi told the story. Apparently, Fritzi saved them. And so did George after she died. The whole thing was spelled out—the mistakes he'd made, how sorry he was, how he'd be home soon. Pat just couldn't believe it.

She ate her stress and sadness, gaining forty-five pounds. It was easier and more comforting to order a pizza or a cheeseburger or Chinese than to cook every night, as she did when George was still there.

———————————

Pat spent the next year building a stack of legal bills. Tens of thousands of dollars' worth. Most months her lawyers gave her a sympathy discount, but it still felt like money she didn't have.

She was left to operate Malört in George's absence, though there wasn't much to do. Sales had tanked, and Florida Distillers' minimum orders were more than Jeppson's could sell.

Pat spent far more of her time staving off George Jr. and Howard Hirsch while navigating a tenuous relationship with David. The four of them hashed out several possible resolutions. In one proposal, David and George Jr. would each get $500,000 from George's estate. Pat and Howard would get $300,000. Pat wasn't a fan of the idea.

In another version, they'd each get the equivalent of $686,250, with a significant portion of Pat's money coming in the form of the condominium, which was valued at close to $300,000. In another, it was $500,000 each. Finally, in April 2000, eight months after George died, they agreed to each pull $575,000 from the estate.

By then the Illinois attorney general's office was watching. All the bickering had made the foundation George envisioned impossible, which led Pat and David to offer $1 million to the Chicago Bar Foundation for educational grants.

The Chicago Bar Foundation contacted the Illinois attorney general's office to review the proposal, and its prodding only raised concerns. At the forefront was a potential conflict of interest for Pat and David as coexecutors of George's estate as they also battled George Jr. and Howard for its contents. The attorney general voided the deal.

In January 2001, almost a year and a half after George's death, Pat, David, George Jr., and Howard ultimately agreed to a resolution that satisfied the attorney general. Each drew $312,500 from George's estate. The Bar Foundation got $2.1 million. Northwestern's law school got its chunk. The rest went to lawyers' fees.

What was never in doubt was the fate of Jeppson's Malört.

George amended his first will, in 1982, to be sure his lifelong hobby wound up with Pat. She was to buy the rights to Carl Jeppson Co. and its sole brand for one hundred dollars each, plus get an amount of cash from the estate needed to buy any existing stock of wormwood and cases of Malört.

For all the months of wrangling and the hundreds of thousands of dollars wasted on lawyers, Malört was the rare subject never to generate an ounce of concern. No one cared. If it had been prosperous, Pat thought, George's sons would have fought for it. It wasn't. So they didn't.

And once the settlement was signed, for the first time in nearly seventy years, Jeppson's Malört no longer belonged to George Brode.

Pat Gabelick owned Jeppson's Malört.

PART II

2001–2011

7

YET SOMEHOW, THE STRANGE DRINK CALLED JEPPSON'S MALÖRT HAS SURVIVED

As a working-class girl growing up in the suburbs west of Chicago, when adulthood still seemed like a hazy eventuality, Pat Gabelick presumed her late fifties would bring grown children and maybe grandchildren, decades of marriage and domestic tranquility, or at least domestic predictability. Instead, she lived quiet days largely alone, functionally a widow, operating a liquor company whose sole product she abhorred, from the spare bedroom of a condominium overlooking the sailboats and joggers traversing Lake Michigan's shore.

When Pat was eighteen, she could have imagined a million scenarios of what life would bring. She was living a million and one, replaying the years in her head. She wondered why she hadn't married when she had the chance, back when she was nineteen, and how different life would have been. She thought about the decisions that ripple through the years, no matter how small they seem at the time. She went to work for George in 1966 not for the job but for the location, in the same building where she worked for the architecture firm. What if she had politely declined the offer from Automatic Canteen and taken the job at the ad agency

for the clarity of vision that it induced. It gave colors extra vibrancy, it sharpened light; it opened up the eyes and endowed the mind with an imaginative wanderlust in a way that other drinks simply didn't. And, importantly for those impoverished artists, it was considerably cheaper than wine.

That lore led to decades of negative associations, including a sickness deemed "absinthism," a disorder of hallucinations, sleeplessness, and convulsions. Absinthe's dark reputation led to widespread prohibitions across Europe and the United States, where a ban went into effect in 1912. The ban would be rescinded in 2007 as studies increasingly cast doubt that wormwood—or absinthe—had any such effects on drinkers, but the uncertainty left Jeppson's Malört skating for decades at the edge of legality.

It was George's greatest source of anxiety after the Food and Drug Administration seized a shipment of the herb as it entered the country in 1981, saying it may have contained a toxic substance it called "absinthe." George got his wormwood through by hiring a lawyer to sign a letter that declared the only customers for the wormwood were "makers of wine, bitters, and vermouth." He preemptively attached the letter to every new shipment.

George never had any idea how much thujone was in Malört, but he worried enough to clip news articles over the years detailing wormwood's brushes with the law. That letter always appeared to solve the problem—until May 2006.

The day her wormwood was held up at the border, Pat was due to meet a cousin for an afternoon movie. She canceled the date and did the only thing she could think to do—drive. Up Lake Shore Drive to Sheridan Road, past George's old house in Glencoe, almost all the way to the Wisconsin border. She put a hundred miles on her car that day. It was the only way to keep calm. The wormwood seizure felt like the end of everything, as if George had entrusted her to nurture his lifelong project and she was about to fail. She couldn't imagine beating the FDA.

Malört was floundering in the market, but she hated the idea of letting the company flicker out. It was a dilemma George faced several times, an obvious off-ramp to shrug and walk away. She couldn't do it. She wasn't even sure why. For herself? For George? He always kept it going. It seemed she should too. She kept his license plate—"GXB"—to honor him. This was the only other way.

Pat and her importer tried tiptoeing around the issue by submitting a letter to the FDA that said, "to the best of our knowledge, there has been no additive of thujone to the shipment." That fooled no one; the FDA noted that thujone occurred naturally in wormwood.

Pat called her probate and tax lawyers. Neither had any idea what to do. She called firms around Chicago, but none had expertise at the intersection of liquor and customs law. One suggested she check with firms in Washington, DC. Pat finally landed at juggernaut McDermott Will & Emery, which charged $600 an hour to recommend she have a bottle of Malört analyzed in a lab.

She grew anxious as the issue drew out, telling her lawyer in early June she needed resolution. "With storage charges in excess of $1,000 and rapidly rising, your $2,000 retainer, Switzerland's original charges, the import costs and the cost of reexporting the goods, I don't believe a company that makes little or no profit can handle much more," she said.

The lawyer told her to send a bottle from the most recent batch, made six months earlier, to a lab in New Jersey to determine whether it fell within allowable levels of thujone—ten parts per million. He was confident Malört would fall well under the threshold but promised nothing.

"Let's hope the numbers hold up in practice," he said by email.

Good news came back in days. Using gas chromatography, the lab concluded that Malört's thujone content was less than one part per million.

And with that, Pat got her wormwood. Production resumed at Florida Distillers. Malört somehow survived yet again.

———————

Then a strange thing happened. Someone noticed.

In the spring of 2007, less than a year after her brush with the FDA, a reader emailed Mark Brown, a twenty-five-year veteran of the

Chicago Sun-Times, with a question: What is this strange and bitter spirit, Jeppson's Malört, that's sold only in Chicago? Brown spent years as an investigative reporter and covering county government. By the time that email arrived, he was a columnist, writing four days a week about whatever moved him—crooked politicians, quirky outsiders, sports, the weather, the rhythms of the city.

He'd never heard of Jeppson's Malört, but Brown knew a good story when he found one. Malört was one of those quirky outsiders. He checked the newspaper's archives and found little coverage beyond George Brode's obituary. He searched the internet but saw no website. No matter. Public records told Brown who owned the company and how to find her.

Pat was surprised to hear from a newspaper reporter, and even more surprised that anyone was curious about Jeppson's Malört. Still, she invited Brown to the condo.

He arrived on a Friday morning. Pat offered a quick tour of the apartment, explaining it had been George's until his death eight years earlier. She showed Brown what functioned as Malört headquarters: her spare bedroom, looking over a canyon of high-rise apartment buildings on Chicago's North Side and, to the east, the swaying blue lake.

Pat struck Brown as both exceedingly polite and phenomenally unlikely to own a liquor company. He wondered how her boss came to leave her the company, whether there was more to the story. He didn't ask; it seemed too personal for an eight-hundred-word newspaper article.

Pat offered Brown a sniff of wormwood from a plastic bag.

"When you breathe it in, it's going to stay in your throat for a while," she said. "I'm just warning you."

Brown didn't think it was so bad, though that may have been because it was older and oxidized, from that ill-fated shipment hung up for weeks in customs—not that Pat dared say anything about that. (Like its cousin cannabis, wormwood loses aromatic punch with age.)

Pat also offered Brown a taste of Malört. He declined, citing the early hour, but promised he'd taste it before publishing.

Two days later the column appeared on page 8 of the Sunday paper, below the headline WHAT DRINK ASKS "ARE YOU MAN ENOUGH?" IT'S A LIQUEUR SO BAD—OR SO WONDERFUL—IT'S ONLY SOLD HERE. Brown opened the only way he could: "There is a drink sold only in Chicago with a taste so vile some bartenders keep a bottle on hand primarily just to serve annoying customers who insist they deserve a free shot of something, as in: 'You want a free drink, pal. Here, try this.'"

Two paragraphs later, he introduced Pat as a business owner who "employs no salesmen, does no advertising and isn't quite sure herself how she stays in business."

"Yet somehow, the strange drink called Jeppson's Malört has survived," Brown wrote.

He noted that "the one-person operation makes just enough money to pay some of her expenses."

It was Malört's first news coverage in decades, or perhaps ever—Pat wasn't sure. She couldn't recall a reporter ever wanting to write about it, even during the decades George ran the operation. Brown did buy a bottle, which he twisted open in his ninth-floor office just before submitting his column. He publicly declared Malört "not that bad," though the truth was he hated it as much as most people. The early impact was tolerable, but the bitterness just lingered. And lingered.

Brown kept that bottle in his office, like the old reporters who faithfully kept whiskey in their desks, figuring it gave him a touch more big-city reporter credibility. The stuff was so vile, though, that no colleague ever stopped by for a shot. Brown certainly couldn't face it again. It just sat there, untouched. Finally, he threw it away.

Malört's flicker of fame came and went. Brown got back to telling the stories of the city. Pat kept her little operation afloat. Neither of them realized that Brown's Sunday column signaled an impending shift for Jeppson's Malört, a shift that had, in fact, already quietly begun.

8

WHAT THE FUCK
WAS THAT?

PAT WOULD COME to think of the early 2000s as the gray period of her life. George was gone. She learned to be a business owner while fretting about her finances. And after years of savoring her city's theaters, symphony, and restaurants, life revolved around a home office where she watched her company's sales plunge with little hope for recovery.

Meanwhile, four miles away, Brad Bolt sat at a bar and slugged down his first taste of Malört. Not so unpleasant, he thought. It was muscular and memorable, like the most bitter grapefruit. Not as bad as everyone said, actually.

It was 2006, about the time Pat worried that her wormwood might not make it past the border and her stubborn little company might finally be doomed. Brad sat at the bar across the street from his apartment in Wicker Park, a neighborhood packed with twentysomethings like himself. He was a bartender, working at several hip, well-regarded restaurants where veteran servers mentioned Malört more than once, warning him, of course, that it was terrible. He never tasted it, though. None of the places he worked carried it.

At dinner that night, at the corner bar along Division Street, there it was. Brad told the bartender he never had it, that he was curious. You don't want to try that, the bartender told him—it's terrible. That only made Brad want to try it more. The bartender poured him a shot.

He had shaken a thousand martinis and poured two thousand whiskey shots. He'd never tasted anything like this.

Among his employers was Del Toro, a dark, cavernous tapas restaurant at a time when such small-plate dining was ascendant. In March 2007 the owner of the restaurant, Terry Alexander, pulled Brad aside to say he was closing Del Toro. In its place, he and a handful of partners would open a bar they planned to call the Violet Hour.

It would have a speakeasy sort of vibe, Terry said; no sign out front and no windows to the street. Just hushed elegance and meticulous cocktails. He asked Brad if he wanted to be behind the bar when doors opened in the coming months.

Brad didn't hesitate. He was in. Three months earlier, Terry clued him in to a New York version of what he'd be attempting in Chicago. The bar was Milk & Honey, opened in January 2000, in a five-story former mah-jongg gambling parlor with a fire escape snaking down its redbrick front. It sat on a garbage-strewn block of Manhattan's Lower East Side described in news coverage over the years as "dark, dangerous" and overrun by "drugs, prostitution, gangs, fights, and theft." There was no sign out front and the one window to the street was deliberately misleading, the word ALTERATIONS painted in an old-fashioned style to evoke the neighborhood's old tailor shops. The visionary behind the operation, twenty-seven-year-old Sasha Petraske, didn't replace or even clean the graffiti-laden door. It could take ten minutes walking up and down Eldridge Street to figure out which storefront hid Milk & Honey.

That was by design. In an interview with the *New York Times* shortly after opening, Petraske, who agreed to an interview with the newspaper on the conditions that Milk & Honey's exact location not be revealed and he be identified only by his first name, said he was trying to cultivate "an idiot-free environment safe from celebrity sycophants and frat boys who read the listings in *Time Out*." The reporter called him a "Holden Caulfield of night life, scorning 'phonies' and crusading against lapsed values."

The only way in was to call the bar with at least twenty minutes' notice with references from previous guests—but first you had to find the phone number. It wasn't listed. After a while, once it rang enough to disturb Petraske as he worked, it would change.

approach with a dash of speakeasy mystery on the second floor of a Japanese restaurant in New York's East Village.

Milk & Honey tied it all together for a new generation with an array of quirks that made its customers not just taste but *feel*. It was a cultural and culinary sea change, though some people found it pompous and verbose: "If submitting to authority in exchange for a drink served with a side of clandestine frisson gets you off ('Oooh, look, you have to ring a DOORBELL and tap your magic ring twice to get in!!'), then by all means: M&H will rock your world," read one review.

For many more, it was the experience they never knew they craved—Brad among them. He marveled at the bartenders' style: the intention, the fluidity of motion, the precise movement. There was no room for error. His evening at Milk & Honey was theatrical but earned every bit of its theater. For all the nights he'd spent in bars, he'd never seen the simple act of measuring out ingredients in a jigger. The majesty and charm were rooted in the simple fact that at the center of it all was a cocktail—and then another and then another after that—made with precision and care. Of course Brad wanted to be part of that in Chicago.

———

When the Violet Hour opened in June 2007, Brad stood behind the bar, dressed in a shirt and tie, hair trimmed tight. Almost all the servers and bartenders were new to the cocktail movement, like Brad, and they were dressed for the moment: crisp pants and some combination of ties, vests, and suspenders for the men and, for the women, vintage dresses. They'd just finished two weeks of intensive training—unusually long for opening a new bar. This wasn't meant to be just any bar.

Chicago finally had its own Milk & Honey, an entry into the stirring speakeasy resurgence that would reach any vaguely ambitious metro area during the next decade—from Philly to Fresno and countless points between.

Like Milk & Honey, the Violet Hour hung no sign out front. It covered over Del Toro's windows to the street. Out front there was a single yellow lightbulb above an ever-changing mural, replaced every few months: a watery blue cityscape, bright flowers, a plain sheet of white, jagged colors, swirly shapes. You had to know it was there—but people quickly knew.

Unlike Milk & Honey, the Violet Hour opened when the modern speakeasy was increasingly understood, still fresh but no longer a secret. Also unlike Milk & Honey, the Violet Hour was spacious and planted in a hip and bustling neighborhood. Wicker Park was still tattered at the edges but hurtling toward gentrification. Going there wasn't strange or scary; it was a sign of cool. Though the Violet Hour was five times the size of Milk & Honey, hour-long lines quickly formed outside, and impatient customers pulled power plays to slip inside.

New York's cocktail scene had grown strong during the previous decade, and it informed much of what happened at the Violet Hour: crystal chandeliers dangling above hardwood floors, heavy blue-gray velvet curtains for a sense of regal exclusivity, and in the foyer and bathrooms, its own set of house rules.

Cell phones were prohibited. "Proper attire" wasn't required but requested ("please, no baseball hats"). Guests were implored not to bring "anyone to The Violet Hour that you wouldn't bring to your mother's house for Sunday dinner." There were "No O-bombs. No Jager-bombs. No bombs of any kind. No Budweiser. No light beer. No Grey Goose. No cosmopolitans."

The similarities to Milk & Honey were informed largely by Toby Maloney, a Violet Hour partner who was also Milk & Honey's first bartender, other than Petraske. His first experience there was as a customer, months after the bar opened. He worked in clubs at the time, mixing endless ruby-red cosmos, bright green appletinis, and bone-dry vodka martinis finished with blue cheese–stuffed olives. A friend clued him in to the genius unfolding at Milk & Honey and invited Toby to join him.

Petraske served Toby a daiquiri—not the standard icy, sugary swill but an elegant, rum-centric take bright with fresh lime juice, poured into a proper coupe. Toby had never tasted anything like it. He was also a bartender—but, he realized, a different sort of bartender. It was like jogging on a treadmill while watching an Olympic sprinter on TV: I'm also doing that but not like *that*.

Toby began visiting Milk & Honey any night he wasn't working, four or five times a week. Petraske embraced his student. When business was slow, they experimented, stirring a gin martini seventeen times, taking its temperature, then stirring it another twenty-nine times and taking its temperature again. They shook the same drink with different sizes and shapes of ice. They sketched out how to build rounds—if an order of four cocktails came in, in what order would you make them to ensure each is pristine by the time they all reach the table?

Toby offered to tend bar on Wednesday nights to give Petraske, operating as Milk & Honey's sole bartender, a sorely needed break. Toby stayed five and a half years. Eventually Milk & Honey grew busy enough to take on new bartenders, and Toby decamped to the next generation of visionary New York bars. He became a face of the movement, preaching an earnest message and telling countless people that no, they could not have a vodka soda or a vodka cranberry or a vodka anything. Vodka was not invited to the cocktail revolution. Plenty of business walked out the door. It didn't matter.

The Violet Hour was a homecoming of sorts for Toby. He was a Colorado native who spent part of his twenties in Chicago; among his first jobs, at twenty-three, was shucking oysters at Soul Kitchen, one of Terry Alexander's earliest restaurants. After five years he followed a girlfriend to New York, where he started working in bars. Terry faithfully visited New York once or twice a year and always headed to the cocktail bar of the moment. More often than not, it seemed Toby was making his drink. When Terry decided to bring that kind of vision to Chicago, Toby was an obvious shepherd.

Both men knew a high-end cocktail bar was no sure thing in Chicago. Though the nation's third-largest city, it remained culturally rooted in Italian beef and greasy pizza, beer and martinis. Despite his occasional doubts, Terry gave Toby license to bring the concept to life as needed. When Toby unveiled the dainty cocktail coupes he planned to use for much of the menu—just like at Milk & Honey—Terry reminded him Chicago was ground zero of oversized martinis, the more olives the better.

"This five-ounce glass is not going to work," he said.

It worked. Early reviews were dazzled by the Violet Hour, if sometimes bemused by the exclusivity. A few weeks after the Violet Hour opened, Mike Sula, who covered food, bars, and restaurants for the alt-weekly *Chicago Reader*, tried visiting at 9:00 PM on a Friday night to check out the city's toniest cocktails, but "it just didn't go down the way I'd hoped," he wrote—which said just as much about what was happening at the Violet Hour as the cocktails it served:

> First we were greeted and carded by the very dapper and welcoming doorman George, who ushered us into [a] spare, unfinished hallway that leads in the bar proper. We had just enough time to glimpse the candlelight drenched, blue velvet draped lounge—a soothing contrast to the chaos on the street—before George whisked us back onto the sidewalk because the bar had hit capacity. He was apologizing and taking down our cell phone number when a young woman broke ranks from the small line that gathered outside the door, brandishing her own phone and demanding George speak to "DeCarlo." (sp?) That's all it took for him to drop us and shift all of his agreeability to the other end of the line, promising the lady would be well taken care of, and bumping her ahead of us to the top of the list. Still George assured us he'd call soon when there'd be space for us, and that he had a "99% success rate" seating patrons.

Sula and his companions spent the next hour and a half drinking their way up Milwaukee Avenue, awaiting a call that never came. They grew ornery as they drank, finally returning to confront George; he insisted they gave him a wrong number. Once inside, Sula and his friends spent twenty minutes waiting for a server, growing grumpier still. They finally left, and Sula's review wound up critiquing the Violet Hour's circus rather than its drinks.

The exclusivity only worked to the Violet Hour's advantage. Even its rules were a hit. Toby believed they were a necessary call to arms, an exhortation to treat this bar and its drinks with unusual respect. It didn't

cool. The Heisler partners surprised him by asking to team up on a new project. They had an opportunity in a one-hundred-year-old building with a first-floor corner bar and two apartments above. It was an ideal canvas to harness the city's fresh energy, juxtaposing top-flight cocktails with an old-school dive in a quiet urban pocket between the hustle of Chicago Avenue and the United Center sports and concert arena a few blocks south. They called it Bar DeVille. It opened in late 2008.

Up front was a bar where Brad mixed cocktails amid an army of bottles and a clacking, clanging antique cash register. In back was something unimaginable at the Violet Hour: a dance floor for the weekend nights when a DJ spun records.

Also unlike the Violet Hour, Brad carried more familiar options, including Jägermeister, light beer—and Jeppson's Malört. Brad and his friends drank it in dive bars after work. Why wouldn't he serve it at *his* dive bar? It wasn't good enough for the Violet Hour, but it sure as hell was for the Violet Hour's mischievous younger sibling down the street. Bar DeVille went through a couple bottles a week, much of it slugged down by Brad and his staff.

The house shot slowly caught on with the weeknight clientele, a mix of neighborhood regulars and restaurant workers just off their shifts. There was no better advertisement for this weird bitter liquor than the folks behind the bar downing shots of it. Weekends drew Chicago's going-out crowd, the twentysomethings looking for a good time. They were slower to Malört but sometimes nudged toward an introduction, especially the one or two times each weekend someone asked for a free birthday shot. In a normal bar, it would be a cheap vodka or maybe a shot of Jameson. At Bar DeVille, out came the Malört. Down the unsuspecting gullet it went.

"What the fuck was that?" more than one astonished customer blurted.

"The same thing we're drinking!" Brad replied. "Cheers!"

"That wasn't a fun shot."

"But we had so much fun watching you."

Brad and his bartenders dissolved into laughter.

Some people got pissy. Others got it. Some were intrigued, asking what *was* that weird thing they just drank? Many people had never heard of it and said they'd be sure never to try it again. Others recognized the name, had heard its legend, and said they actually sort of liked it—or that it at least wasn't as bad as they'd heard.

Brad was always glad to hear that. He never shocked customers with Malört to be mean. He thought Malört was interesting and fun. It was uniquely Chicago, and he took pride in running a Chicago bar. For all its bitterness and intensity, he enjoyed Malört—or at least appreciated it. He wanted other people to appreciate it too.

9

I HAVE HEARD IT DESCRIBED AS "IF YOU DRANK WATER OUT OF AN ASH TRAY"

SOMETHING WAS HAPPENING, and it was bigger than any one bar, one person, one cocktail, or one shot. It was something in the wind, a thousand tiny ripples cresting into a wave.

Just as the world had shifted once under Malört's feet—Chicago's turn from blue collar to white, the demise of its neighborhood bars and well-paid, working-class jobs—it moved again.

The change came over decades, starting as early as the 1970s and '80s, accelerating in the '90s and, by the early twenty-first century, it was a city reborn from its predominantly working-class past. Neighborhoods once packed with generations of middle-class families filled with young professionals and redevelopment. The shift ushered in an appetite for fresh choice, new options, and a coffee shop seemingly on every corner.

The reimagined approaches to eating and drinking included farm-to-table restaurants, built on dishes rooted in ingredients sourced with environmental, economic, nutritional, and social focus. A new generation of chefs shook off decades of presumption that destination dining had to be rooted in French, Italian, or steakhouse cuisines; instead, the young chefs tapped into their own narratives, bringing the foods and flavors of their families into their dining rooms. Farmers' markets offered fresh alternatives to the postwar rise of processed conglomerate foods; the number of markets more than doubled between 2000 (fewer than three thousand) and 2011 (more than seven thousand). Foods rarely found at mainstream grocery stores a generation earlier became heartland staples—from blue cheese to hummus, salsa to sriracha.

The mainstream had to take note. Burger King launched a veggie burger in 2002; McDonald's followed a year later. As sales of cow's milk stalled and milk alternatives surged, Starbucks added soy milk to a handful of stores in the late 1990s; by 2015 it stocked coconut milk in more than twelve thousand US locations. Organic food did $10 billion in retail sales in the United States in 2001; ten years later the figure approached $30 billion.

The shift ushered in an era of buzzwords. Along with "farm-to-table" came the rise of "local" and "craft." "Craft," in particular, became prolific. There was craft pizza and craft soda. Craft doughnuts and craft cupcakes. Craft beer reinvigorated the American beer industry, which grew from fewer than one hundred breweries in the 1970s to nearly five thousand in 2015 (a figure that would eventually approach ten thousand).

Ever more people described themselves as "foodies" as dining pushed deeper into media and culture—the birth of the Food Network, the ascendance of celebrity chefs, and a shift from not only what we ate but also what entertained us: *Top Chef, Chopped, Jiro Dreams of Sushi, Super Size Me*. New ways of eating led to new appreciation of flavors. Western palates came to understand the savory depth of umami. Sweet was king of the twentieth century, Americans gorging on dozens of pounds of sugar per year; but after peaking in 1999, sugar consumption entered two decades of decline. As menus grew more thoughtful and taste buds more nuanced, the groundwork was laid for a new generation to embrace bolder flavors.

Kale, for instance, had always been there, mostly as a bitter afterthought, but between 2007 and 2012, production rose nearly 60 percent as the number of kale farms grew from fewer than a thousand to twenty-five hundred. It was at Walmart and McDonald's. Kale's prominence on restaurant menus soared, and Whole Foods sold more than twenty-two thousand bunches of it every day. It was an unlikely rise for a brittle, bitter vegetable long relegated to adornment status at countless salad bars—but it tracked with where tastes were headed. Brussels sprouts would soon follow. Restaurateurs who couldn't have fathomed selling such a bitter vegetable in the '90s saw it become their most popular side dish.

Drinkers, too, embraced bigger flavors: peaty Scotch grew into an American sensation. After decades of decline even steeper than bourbon, bold, spicy rye whiskey stunned industry observers by growing 20 percent in 2006, then 30 percent in 2007. Intensely bitter India pale ale became an engine of craft beer and the industry's top-selling style. Fernet-Branca, a bitter Italian liqueur, became a hit in the bars of San Francisco. Drinkers were not only open to new things and challenging flavors after decades of bland uniformity—they craved them.

George didn't know he was doing it. Neither did Pat. But simply keeping Malört alive for close to a hundred years allowed the world to make sense of it. Malört never changed to please the masses. The masses changed to understand Malört.

––––––––––

Just as important as how a nation ate and drank was how a nation talked about how it ate and drank, and the shift dovetailed immaculately with the rise of Jeppson's Malört.

Social media.

The experience of eating and drinking was no longer confined to the moment, then only a fond memory, and maybe a recommendation to family or friends. Suddenly, we could capture those experiences and share them in real time with vast audiences—people we knew well, people we hadn't seen in ages, and even complete strangers. In 2007 that's exactly what happened to Malört on Flickr, an early medium for sharing photos.

It started with Ryan Bastianelli, a thirty-five-year-old avionics technician who helped maintain the electrical systems on United Airlines planes. He discovered Jeppson's Malört one day after work and, in true Malört fashion, by mistake.

He'd talked that day with a coworker about obscure liquors. The coworker mentioned akvavit, another Scandinavian spirit steeped in herbs. Ryan was eager to try it and stopped at a liquor store on the way home. He couldn't remember the word *akvavit*, though, and told the sales clerk he was looking for some kind of Scandinavian liquor made with caraway. The clerk didn't know what he meant and handed him a bottle of Jeppson's Malört.

Ryan brought it to his apartment on the West Side of Chicago and poured a shot. He was stunned by what he tasted—so bad he insisted his wife try it. She also thought it was awful. *Who would even buy this?* he wondered.

That question only intrigued Ryan because, clearly, *someone* must buy it. But who? And why? The whole equation was a mystery. The label was odd and dated. The booklet dangling from its neck was clearly a relic of another era (and in fact Pat would soon phase it out as the rare cost that she could save). Ryan was especially amused by the line "only 1 out of 49 men will drink Jeppson Malört after the first 'shock-glass.'"

One in *forty-nine*?

A *shock-glass*?

He grabbed his phone and snapped a photo of the bottle to show everyone at work the next day. It felt like he stumbled onto an absurd secret. He couldn't wait to share.

No one had heard of it except for an older guy named George, who knew exactly what it was. George said he worked in the steel mills in the '60s and '70s, and at the end of a hot, grueling week, he and his buddies headed directly to the bar. They spent hours upon hours drinking. They'd stagger home, wake up hungover, eat breakfast, and then head back to the bar. The first thing they drank? A shot of Jeppson's Malört. It was their medicine. It helped get them right. Then they started drinking again.

George's story only intrigued Ryan more. This weird stuff had that kind of history?

Ryan still thought Malört was terrible, but it enthralled him. He began bringing it to parties to share with friends, gleefully announcing, "I invented bringing Malört to parties!" which, among his generation of Chicago drinkers, he very well may have. The looks on his friends' faces

not to notice Malört stirring to relevance around him, especially among Bar DeVille bartenders.

It piqued a reporter's curiosity. As Sula would eventually write, he wondered if "some of my favorite bartenders—employing fresh juices, fine spirits, and the trained mixologist's keen sense of balance and proportion—could come up with cocktails that would actually redeem Malört from its unsavory reputation."

He would soon learn that it was already happening, with approaches both elevated and lowbrow. A suburban sports bar, Brixie's, was fascinated by Malört, ordering about a case a month for what Sula called "a concerted two-year campaign by doorman Dan Marco and his younger brother, Tim, to devise as many Malort-based concoctions and deflower as many Malort virgins as they can." The brothers loved both Malört's brashness and its power to shock. Their goal, Dan Marco told Sula, was to create "the nastiest thing we could."

They came up with plenty of nasty, including the Malasco (a shot of Malört spiked with Tabasco), Brixie's Biledriver (Malört and orange juice), the Malörtarita (with triple sec and lime juice), and the Scandalous Scandinavian (Malört, soda, and a dash of Angostura bitters).

Meanwhile, one of Chicago's most esteemed bartenders, Charles Joly, spent months trying to build nuanced cocktails at his bar, the Drawing Room, from Malört's inherent lack of nuance. As a young bargoer in the 1990s, Joly thought of Malört as "stomach bile and dirt," he liked to say. As his palate grew sharper, so did his understanding of Malört, which came to seem earthy, akin to bitter grapefruit pith. Add a little sugar and a little lemon, he realized, and Malört became an immaculate bitter grapefruit component. He landed on the Bukowski—the irascible writer whom the irascible spirit most reminded him of—built with one and a half ounces of Malört and half an ounce of Drambuie; shaken with orange and lemon juice, honey syrup, and basil leaves; then served on the rocks.

Sula wondered: *Could any of this actually work?*

And who better than Pat Gabelick to decide?

Sula found her phone number and pitched her on the idea of a bar crawl. He would take her to some of the city's best bars, helmed by some of the best bartenders, and at each stop they would try a cocktail (or two) made with Jeppson's Malört. Pat would pick the winner.

She was pleased to hear from Sula, and thought his idea sounded fun—but she didn't understand why anyone would make a cocktail with Malört. Years earlier, George's "Are you man enough to drink our two-fisted liquor?" booklets included cocktail recipes that no one took seriously. No one was meant to take them seriously. It was just George's silly marketing.

But now, Sula said, bartenders were doing the very thing George envisioned all those years ago. It made no sense to Pat. Who would want to drink a cocktail made with Malört? Why would anyone care about Malört at all? Did Sula have any idea how bad sales were? He insisted: Malört was gaining resonance in some of Chicago's coolest bars. People were talking about it, mixing it, hoisting late-night shots, and turning it into a civic badge of pride.

Pat heard the words. She didn't believe them.

Sula kept talking, kept trying to convince her to see for herself. Finally, Pat agreed. She considered herself a nice person, and she wanted to be nice.

A few days later, Sula pulled up outside Pat's lakefront condo in his white 1994 Toyota Tercel. It was an unusually warm March afternoon. Pat came down in a light jacket and matching pants.

Sula knew Malört's vague backstory: George Brode owned it for decades, Pat was his secretary, and George left her the company when he died. Like Mark Brown a couple years earlier, Sula wondered if there was more to the story. He poked at the narrative, wondering if Pat would share details. Pat didn't offer. Sula didn't push. He figured his article would be good enough without the answer, and he didn't want to risk derailing things.

He whisked her to a world just a few miles away, which Pat had no idea existed: a neighborhood bar where cocktails were built with precision and care. It was another world from the dingy, smoky, man-packed dives where Malört hung on for decades.

In this case it was the Whistler, a cocktail bar doubling as a small live music venue that had opened just a few months earlier in Logan Square, another gentrifying Chicago neighborhood. At the bar stood Paul McGee, the Whistler's thickly bearded co-owner and lead bartender. He was expecting them; Sula arranged for each bartender to be ready with a Malört cocktail in mind.

McGee stunned Pat with the first curveball of the journey: he already served a Malört cocktail at the Whistler.

McGee had worked in bars since the age of nineteen, first in his hometown of Houston, then in Las Vegas, for chef Wolfgang Puck. He never heard of Malört until arriving in Chicago in 2008, a year before opening the Whistler. A salesman for one of his liquor distributors, Brian Vaughan, mentioned it. Vaughan said it was a local oddity that wasn't particularly popular and seemed semi-mothballed, with no sales or marketing behind it. No one knew much about the woman who owned it, he said. Or why it was made in Florida. He called it "kitschy."

Even so, it was a rite of passage around town, Vaughan said, and the bartenders respected it as a local staple. When he worked at a legendary whiskey bar in town called Delilah's during the 1990s, it was nicknamed "the birthday shot." A special day deserved a special shot. That, Vaughan said, was what Malört was. McGee might not sell much of it, but it would at least lend credibility to his back bar.

Vaughan poured McGee a taste. McGee sniffed it and raised his eyebrow. He threw back the shot. It was all the terrible things. Thin body. So ablaze it reminded him of pure ethanol. And, of course, extraordinarily bitter. Some balancing sweetness would have helped, McGee thought. He didn't like it—but he could appreciate it. It was local and it offered a point of view. A bartender's job was to curate an experience, to be a cultural ambassador for whoever sat at the bar, and he could imagine how this bitter spirit might do that. Sure, McGee said. He'd take a bottle.

Soon after the Whistler opened, two neighbors spied the bottle behind the bar and knew exactly what it was. One of them challenged McGee to use it in a cocktail. The idea seemed part joke and part dare—but also sincere. Could an elite cocktail mixer, one who worked for one of the world's most famous chefs, figure out how to incorporate such a polarizing flavor into a unified whole? McGee didn't dwell long on the challenge. He thought immediately of a Negroni, a classic bitter cocktail typically made with equal parts gin, sweet vermouth, and Campari, a bitter Italian liqueur made with an infusion of herbs and fruit that was a more accessible cousin to Malört. McGee swapped out Campari for Malört. The regulars were pleased.

"They both loved it, and subsequently named it the Golden Eel after a Ween song by the same name," McGee told Sula. "They thought the drink was good, but kinda messed up, and so is Ween."

McGee thought the creation was just OK. He wouldn't dare add it to the menu but did file it away for the rare request for a Malört cocktail—which happened more than he expected. McGee later wondered if he could come up with a refreshing version of a Malört cocktail and landed on a riff on the Paloma: silver tequila, half an ounce of Malört, orange and lime juice, finished with spicy ginger beer.

With Malört's owner standing before him, McGee mixed both cocktails for her. Pat seemed kind and grandmotherly, though in a plain-talking, no-nonsense kind of way; she was clear that she was no fan of her own brand and not particularly eager to try the cocktails. She seemed to be there mostly to humor Sula. McGee was amused by that.

Pat took a sip of both. That was enough.

They went on to the Violet Hour. Pat marveled at the elegance. She was surprised such a place would have anything to do with Malört. It didn't, really; Malört still wasn't behind the bar or used in any Violet Hour cocktails. Even so, Toby Maloney couldn't resist Sula's invite to take part in the competition.

Toby was out of town the day Pat and Sula arrived, but another bartender, Stephen Cole, had two recipes ready. One was his and the other was Toby's. Cole's was called the Michigan Cutter, which combined an ounce of Malört with bittersweet Italian digestif Amaro Montenegro, plus lemon juice, simple syrup, a dash of orange bitters, and egg white to add creamy texture. He topped it with 7-Up for sweetness. The Amaro, Sula wrote, "rounded off the Malort and mitigated its shock, making the bitter finish enjoyable." Pat simply appreciated the presence of egg white.

"As a woman, it makes it a little more fun to drink," she said. "Something that's frothy like that."

Toby's cocktail was, like McGee's, also a riff on a Negroni: a quarter ounce of Malört, two ounces of gin, an ounce and a half of sweet vermouth, a quarter ounce of Campari, and oils from an orange peel ignited and squeezed across the top. He called it the Ukrainian Negroni, in honor of the Ukrainian Village neighborhood down the street from the Violet Hour, whose dive bars had offered Toby his first taste of Malört nearly twenty years earlier. Sula called it "the booziest and perhaps most challenging—and yet most balanced—cocktail we tasted."

Pat was, once again, no fan. She preferred her white wine.

Finally, they reached Bar DeVille, where Brad Bolt waited behind the bar. Sula had asked him to be part of the competition weeks earlier. Brad didn't hesitate. He thought it was a brilliant idea that could go horribly awry. At least the playing field would be level—everyone hampered by the same ingredient—so he figured the fun was worth the risk. He wouldn't have been surprised if Pat hated them all.

His immediate thought was to make a drink that tasted of bitter grapefruit. Within a couple days he came up with a blend of equal parts Malört, Beefeater gin, St-Germain elderflower liqueur, and fresh-squeezed lemon juice, finished with a grapefruit-peel twist. He called it the Hard Sell— because getting someone to drink a Malört cocktail would be just that.

Pat took a sip. She brightened. It was, finally, the one cocktail of the day she enjoyed. The rest of the ingredients, especially the elderflower liqueur, overwhelmed the taste of the Malört.

A few weeks later, Sula's article ran on page 15 of the *Reader*, the newspaper's lead food and drink story of the week, below the headline SHOT OF MALÖRT, HOLD THE GRIMACE. Any press was good press, Pat figured, and she set aside a couple of copies. It seemed likely to be the pinnacle of Malört in the social conversation.

The story wasn't quite over, though. A month after the article was published, the Hard Sell tied for first place in a monthly cocktail competition sponsored by St-Germain. Brad flew to New York to compete against a dozen other bartenders for a weeklong trip to Paris. Among the judges was the legendary Dale DeGroff.

Brad didn't win—DeGroff complained that Malört was too bitter—but Brad did prove that it *could* be taken seriously. Even Pat liked the drink. Sula asked if she thought a broader, more meaningful shift might be underway.

"I'm hopeful," Pat said. "But I'm a glass-half-empty kind of person."

———————————

The glass remained half empty. Sure, a few bartenders experimented with Jeppson's Malört, and some people made fun of it on the internet. But the sales were the sales. After cratering to 2008's all-time low, they crept up in 2009—then slipped again in 2010.

At nearly seventy years old, savings account dwindling, Pat seemed unlikely to ever support herself with Jeppson's Malört. She was able to take a little more than $30,000 as salary from the company—less than she made as its secretary. That also seemed unlikely to change.

What the sales didn't show Pat was something more important than how much Malört she sold: who was buying it. The spreadsheet cataloged fifteen hundred cases, but it was no longer fifteen hundred cases of a dying brand. It was fifteen hundred cases of discovery.

The audience morphed from crusty dive bar regulars to a new generation of young and adventurous drinkers who hung out in hip bars and trawled social media late at night. They brought joy and wonder to their Malört drinking. They wanted to revel in it, to talk about it, to share it with friends, to laugh at it, to laugh with it.

They used Malört to consecrate moments—the beginning of a night, the end of a night, birthdays, bachelor parties, weddings, running into old friends, a favorite team winning the championship. They asked for it in bars, from bartenders used to serving old men watching the Cubs game, not roving bands of twentysomethings in ironic T-shirts. They discovered it while traveling to Chicago, failing to believe what they were tasting, then stuffing it into their suitcases because they couldn't buy it back home.

A Monday-night Malört club sprung up at a suburban sports bar. A public radio podcast in search of the "worst liquor in the world" settled on Malört as its "winner." Through choked laughter, one taster sputtered: "That is so awful . . . there's nothing redeeming about that . . . that is horrible . . . oh my god . . . seriously this is . . . the most unpleasant thing ever." At least people were talking about it.

Some of these developments reached Pat. Most did not. There was *still* no company website, no social media accounts, and not even an email address. There seemed to be no reason to connect to the wider world—though there was. If she was ever to understand, someone would need to find her. And in 2011, someone found her.

11

PAT AND PETER

THE *CHICAGO READER* published every Thursday, showing up in thick stacks in coffee shops and grocery stores and yellow metal boxes across Chicago. Peter Strom always picked one up as soon as it hit the streets. It was a cultural touchstone, packed with some of the city's most incisive investigative journalism, plus the latest music listings, movie reviews, and news of what to eat and drink. Peter flipped through the new issue on a cool April afternoon in 2009. On page 15, he paused. It was as if the heavens opened. A mystery was solved.

Peter was a Chicago native from a tight-knit Swedish American family. As a boy he heard of some terrible liquor in the community that he should never drink. He didn't think much more about it. He also heard of some liquor available only in Chicago, which seemed odd since a distillery hadn't operated in the city in decades. He figured it must be imported from Poland, something for the city's massive Polish population. Reading about Pat's bar crawl told him that, in fact, the two things were the same. Both were Jeppson's Malört. Peter was an ardent fan of Chicago bars and its drinking culture, yet he'd somehow never heard of it.

It was a thrilling discovery, a jumble of what interested him most: Chicago history, the city's legacy of alcohol production, and Swedish American culture. At the center of it all were questions, so many questions. What actually was this stuff? How had it survived so long? How did this woman come to own and operate it, seemingly on her own? Within an hour, Peter walked out of his neighborhood liquor store cradling a bottle of Jeppson's Malört.

He brought it to a friend's apartment that night and, standing in her kitchen, twisted off the cap. The bright, herbal aroma seemed promising. They each took a shot, and Peter was delighted at what he found. He liked it. He really liked it. It was bitter and astringent, but a fascinating flavor he didn't know existed, almost impossible to describe. It scratched an itch he didn't know he had.

Peter kept buying Malört and kept drinking it. He kept bottles at home. He drank shots in bars. He'd pack two bottles, if not three, for long weekends in Michigan or Wisconsin with friends. Most of those friends found it disgusting. A handful saw what he saw. A joke blossomed among his social circle: Peter loved Malört like few people loved anything. When two friends got married at the Swedish American Museum, the bride implored Peter *not* to bring a bottle of Malört. So he brought it in a brown paper bag. The groom had quietly asked him to.

Peter was fascinated by the history of the stuff as much as the liquid in the bottle, yet the history was so hazy and incomplete. He searched the internet and found little. He figured it was a Swedish story and a Swedish American story and a Chicago story—but the pieces didn't quite fit.

Peter became curious to reach out to the woman who owned Malört. Perhaps she could unlock the mystery in a ten-minute phone conversation. In the *Reader* article, though, she seemed like she didn't want to be bothered, someone resigned to Malört's fate as an eternal afterthought. Maybe something about being a "glass-half-empty kind of person." Besides, who was he to get in touch with her? What could he offer other than his fandom?

———————

In spring 2011, more than two years after Sula's article, Peter finally resolved to find Pat. He'd talked himself out of it many times. Now a feeling gnawed at him. She had to be nearing seventy. If she really was resigned to Malört's grim fate, his favorite shot might not be around much longer. He hated to think of showing up at the liquor store one day to find it gone forever. So he decided to reach out. If nothing else, maybe its history could be saved.

There was no obvious route to finding Pat, so Peter contacted the one person he knew had access: Mike Sula. On a Wednesday evening in late May, Peter wrote to the *Reader*'s general email address, typing in the subject line "Attention: Mike Sula, Malört."

> Dear Mike,
> I've really enjoyed your articles on Malört. Your first article had me running to my neighborhood liquor store—several bottles later (plus 2 bottles of the Swedish Baska Droppar) and I'm a huge fan (along with a <u>very small</u> number of my friends)!

Peter said he wanted to tell Pat how much he enjoyed Malört. He also said he was "a bit of a history nerd" and wanted to know more of its backstory. He concluded with a window into his two years of Malört devotion: embracing it as a gag and a badge of honor, and using it to celebrate the Chicago Blackhawks 2010 Stanley Cup championship. Best of all, bartenders rarely charged for it—because who would want to pay for such a thing?

> Oh man, Mike, the pain and hilarity I've witnessed across the city over the past two years since your article first appeared! It's been great! From drinking with washed-up baseball players to tricking some sad-sack yuppie into drinking it with me after the hawks won the cup, I've really come to enjoy (and mostly for free, at that) the bitterness in the spirit of Chicago!

Sula hadn't talked to Pat in more than a year, though he did keep writing about Malört, including a piece about his own homemade version ("no apparent ill effects beyond a slight headache and the persistent Malorty bitterness in the back of my mouth," he wrote). He dug up her number and called to say a guy named Peter Strom wanted to know

He didn't hear back. Peter figured that would be the end of their correspondence. He would go on drinking Malört and loving it, wondering about its past and hoping for its future. Then, three weeks later, a curt email arrived:

Please let me know where and when you would like to meet.

Pat didn't even bother signing it. The terseness made Peter think she responded grudgingly—but at least she responded. And the truth was, Pat *did* respond grudgingly. Who was this Peter Strom and what was his endgame? But few others were interested in her time or in Jeppson's Malört. So why not?

They agreed to meet at 3:00 PM the following Wednesday at a Swedish restaurant down the street from Peter's apartment for coffee and dessert. Pat arrived early; she was early to most things. She parked outside the restaurant in her 1998 black Lincoln Continental—George's old car, still bearing his "GXB" license plates—and watched customers shuffle in and out. A silver-haired man hobbled in with a cane. Pat figured it must be Peter Strom. Surely no one much younger could be so curious about Malört.

She walked in and was stunned at who approached her: a man young enough to be her son. Peter was twenty-nine, lean and nice looking, with a mop of brown hair. He was a Chicago native who graduated from a Lutheran high school, then North Park College, a private school with Scandinavian heritage less than a mile from his childhood home that three generations of his father's family had attended. Peter spent the decade after college as a renaissance man of sorts. He worked as a swim instructor, a waiter, an assistant archivist at his alma mater, a Wrigley Field fan ambassador, and a Chicago River canoe guide. For fun, he wrote poetry and surfed on Lake Michigan. Now his full-time job was as a church custodian, working for his father.

Pat seemed terse and wary at first, and Peter didn't blame her, but they quickly developed a rapport. Pat admitted she expected an old man. Peter joked he'd been accused of being an old man his whole life. They had plenty to talk about, more than either expected. Peter had no hesitation talking to people a generation or two older; it was how he grew up. Pat was of Czech descent; Peter was largely Swedish, but his lone non-Swedish grandparent was Czech. They connected over that. They'd both spent summer weekends in southwestern Michigan—Peter growing up, Pat with George. Peter's uncle was a lifelong bachelor with a crew of friends who struck Peter as quintessential Chicago characters, people seemingly around forever with stories about Muddy Waters and Studs Terkel and Nelson Algren. Pat reminded him of one of them.

Finally, they talked about Malört. From his first sip, Peter said, he was desperate to know more. Pat was surprised to hear that. For so long, it seemed no one cared. Peter said he cared plenty. He had lived in Sweden for eighteen months and used his command of the language to research what he could during the last couple of years. The document she sent connected a few dots, he said, but it also raised questions. Did she have more information? More documents? More memories? She said there was once a trove of information, but she threw much of it away when George died. Peter winced. A few boxes remained, though, she said—mostly George's old marketing materials that she didn't have the heart to toss.

Well, he said, whatever remained might be worth archiving. Jeppson's Malört was a slice of Chicago history, and it deserved to live. Peter told her about the archive at North Park University, where he worked for two years after graduation. It was a school founded by Swedish immigrants and operated the Center for Scandinavian Studies, a natural place to preserve the history of Jeppson's Malört. He suggested they reconvene at her apartment in a week and survey the memorabilia. Pat said she wasn't sure she had enough to be worth cataloging. Peter said it wasn't about having a lot—just preserving what was there.

Archiving Malört's history seemed silly to Pat, but the young man across the table, drinking cup after cup of coffee, seemed so gracious and sincere, enthusiastic and curious. They talked for hours, and Pat felt as if she could have talked more. The next day she emailed Peter to thank him for the conversation. They agreed to another meeting.

Peter drove to Pat's lakefront apartment the following Friday to dig through the boxes on her office shelves. He was dazzled by the views; he'd lived in the city his entire life but never been in one of its lakefront condos. Though Pat tried harnessing his expectations, there was plenty to excite him: decades of George's letters to distributors and bar owners, his ridiculous old advertisements, even his head shots—plump face, receding hairline, wire glasses, cocksure smile—as a young liquor executive.

Pat had no attachment to any of it. Even the photos weren't the George she knew. Yet Peter thanked her profusely, saying the project might help him get work as a historian or an archivist. He was unfathomably excited about Malört. That charmed Pat. He asked nothing in return. That made her trust him.

They visited the North Park archives. Pat was impressed by the sophistication of the operation, down to the constant tabs on the room's humidity. The archivist said North Park would be happy to take the materials. All Pat needed to do was sign over ownership of the documents—though she might want to make copies for herself first.

That was the moment Peter knew Jeppson's Malört was not about to die. Pat turned steely and skeptical, striking Peter for the first time as a business owner rather than simply a kind older lady cluelessly fumbling through ownership of a weird brand of liquor. Pat wasn't ready to sign anything away. In her hesitation Peter saw that Malört was still *hers*. It was too soon to hand it to history.

Peter's vision immediately spun another direction: rather than mothball and memorialize, invest and expand. If interest in Malört was rising—look no further than the young man rifling through the boxes in Pat's office—it might keep growing. Maybe Pat should build a website to sell T-shirts and replicas of George's old marketing materials. They were cheeky and dated but offered a retro charm that underscored Malört's history.

Pat wasn't ready to give up on Malört, but she doubted T-shirts and posters were worth the effort. The sales were still the sales. Peter insisted: the sales *weren't* simply the sales. From his time in the bars, he sensed momentum shifting. This was a way to find out for sure and, if he was right, to push things forward.

Still, she was skeptical. For more than a decade, she steered Malört in one direction: straight. No deviations. She did things just as George showed her. Most beer and liquor companies craved growth; Pat only wanted to hang on. By trying to grow, or change anything at all, she worried she might kill the thing she'd been charged with protecting.

She sat with the idea for a bit and emailed her lawyer to ask if selling T-shirts and posters required additional business licenses, or if the tax burden might be a problem. She didn't tell Peter, but she thought about paying him a small commission if they decided to go ahead.

"There does seem to be a little uptake in Jeppson's popularity," she told the lawyer by email. "NPR had a 'worst-tasting liquor' contest and Jeppson won. I had a few calls from around the country asking if they could purchase a bottle. The *Reader* and the *Sun-Times* have done articles in the last few years. My sales may have increased a few hundred cases, but I can't really be sure for another year or so."

Finally, Pat agreed. She told Peter it was time to move forward, and if she was to move forward, would he help? She was even willing to codify the relationship by granting the title he asked for, one George never could have fathomed: Carl Jeppson Company intern.

12

PETER AND CHRIS

Two MONTHS EARLIER, Peter Strom was trying to find the guts to email Pat. He found them, and now he was in her inner circle. Hell, he *was* the inner circle.

He wasn't on Malört's payroll, but Pat made clear it wasn't because she was cheap. There just wasn't enough money to go around. If he wanted to comb the archives, he was welcome. If he wanted to help steer the company with fresh ideas and youthful perspective, well, she needed the help. His head spun with elation.

Peter resolved not to overstep his bounds, or at least try not to. He was excited and full of ideas. But it was Pat's company. He was just the fresh pair of eyes. He had Pat's trust. He didn't want to lose it.

Yet the fact remained that Malört was fragile, adrift, and stuck in the past. That was particularly true online. It wasn't just that Pat failed to harness the internet's sprawling possibility—it was that she left it for the rest of the world. Not only was the Malört Face Flickr account generating yuks (and yucks) on Malört's behalf, someone also started a Jeppson's Malört Facebook page in 2008. In 2010 the same thing happened on Twitter. Both accounts straddled a line between fan appreciation and voice of the company—which was it? It was hard to tell.

The accounts were sophomoric and profane, and they positioned Malört as an edgy outsider doubling as Chicago's coolest inside joke.

Both built sizable audiences and proved Malört was no longer just for old men in old-man bars. The Twitter account was particularly spicy:

> FACT: The wormwood in Malort is proven to treat indigestion, vaginitis, and stomach worms. Springbreakers, pack accordingly. (April 16, 2011)

> It is currently 98.6°F in Chicago. If I were you, I would take this opportunity to say "It's hot as BALLS" with zero sense of irony. (July 20, 2011)

> When my kid turns 5, I'm going to give him a shot of Malört and scream, "ALL ALCOHOL TASTES LIKE THIS!" I'm going to be such a good dad. (October 5, 2011)

Both accounts built the sort of engagement that every brand craved but most struggled to cultivate. Peter found them amusing enough, largely striking the right tone to appeal to a younger, edgier crowd—but who knew where things might go. Social media was still young, but no other alcohol company, no company at all, would allow some faceless person, or people, to curate a digital identity on its behalf. When Peter tried to explain his concern to Pat, she didn't see the urgency.

Among the first things Peter did in his role as Carl Jeppson Company intern was to widen the inner circle. He called his old pal Chris.

Peter and Chris Depa grew up five doors apart in North Mayfair, an idyllic Chicago neighborhood packed with young families and stately brick bungalows. They were always together as kids, playing video games, trading comic books, and watching movies.

As a married father of three, Chris moved to the suburbs—as it turned out, not only the same suburb where Pat lived thirty years earlier with her mother and grandmother but on the same street. The coincidence made Pat feel as if it all made sense, that meeting these young men at this moment in Malört's trajectory was meant to be. Chris's expertise was web design and marketing, and there were few things Jeppson's Malört needed more than web design and marketing.

Peter and Chris convened on a late summer evening in 2011 in the basement of Chris's parents' house. Chris was familiar with Jeppson's Malört but didn't know much of its backstory. He was hardly surprised at his old friend's new infatuation. That was Peter. He was smart, loyal, and fanatical about the things that interested him, even as a kid. At the age of ten, Peter discovered *Star Trek*. He became so engrossed that Chris begged him to talk about anything else.

Passion for *Star Trek* had morphed several times, and now it was Jeppson's Malört. This time Peter had Chris's full attention as he explained all he'd learned in recent weeks: Pat worked for George; she inherited the company and now she was older, alone, and operating it as if still in the 1970s. He explained a vision where Malört's gross-out factor might seize people's attention, but they would become loyal customers with sincere appreciation for the brand and its history. Malört was far more interesting than anyone knew. With decades of heritage, it was a cultural time capsule telling the story of immigration and assimilation.

There was no way to prove it, at least from Peter's vantage, but it just *felt* as if Malört was on the upswing. For two years it was his curiosity and passion, and in the bars he frequented—neighborhood joints full of middle-class regulars—Malört increasingly seemed to be part of the social fabric. Opportunity abounded. To seize it, the conclusion was obvious: Carl Jeppson Company had to catch up to the moment. Quickly.

Right away Chris saw what Peter saw. He didn't have the same enthusiasm for the product itself, but for a marketing and brand expert, it was a dream opportunity, a rare intersection of blank slate, one-of-a-kind product and passionate subculture. Malört elicited reaction and stirred emotion. There were so many stories to tell.

Chris didn't necessarily envision Jeppson's Malört as a long-term piece of his life; he had a full-time job, dabbled in freelance work, and had two kids. Steering such a product into the twenty-first century would be a once-in-a-career challenge, though. The cult following meant something there connected with people—and that meant it could connect with more, perhaps many more. First, Peter and Chris agreed, they needed to prioritize needs.

Facebook and Twitter were lost causes for the moment, but just as baffling as leaving those for the general public to control was the absence of a Jeppson's Malört website. Chris immediately searched for its most obvious home, Jeppsonsmalort.com. It was still available—and sheer luck that whoever operated the social media accounts hadn't also grabbed the URL. Chris whipped out his credit card and started typing the numbers into his laptop. He was buying it.

"Wait, do we need to ask Pat?" Peter said.

"If we don't buy it, someone else will," Chris said.

They told her the next day what they'd done. Pat didn't mind a bit. It cost less than twenty dollars, so it seemed fine.

Two weeks later Pat thanked Peter with a letter on Carl Jeppson Company letterhead—the same letterhead George used for decades, bearing a silhouette of a Swedish Viking ship crossing the ocean.

"Spending your time working as an intern on the Jeppson's Malort project is one thing," she wrote, "but I don't want you to spend your own money."

She enclosed a check for fifty dollars to reimburse Peter for the web address and "perhaps a little of your gas" to get to Chris's house and back. She said she hoped they could get together for a cheeseburger and a Manhattan or two soon with Peter's girlfriend of several years.

Peter was excited for the fifty dollars but even more pleased to have a check bearing his name from the Carl Jeppson Company. In an era before remote bank deposits, he tried figuring out how to get the money while keeping the check; he wanted to frame it. Ultimately, he wanted the money more, so he deposited it into his bank account and settled for keeping the check stub.

———————————

As Peter learned more about George Brode, a question about the Jeppson's Malört story gnawed at him: Did Carl Jeppson actually exist?

Peter admired what he knew of George. His corny humor reminded Peter of one of his grandfathers, and Pat's tales of George's creativity always made Peter smile. Yet George's marketing zeal also seemed a plausible source for a fictitious Swedish immigrant to sell an oddly bitter Swedish spirit.

Look no further than the booklets dangling from Malört bottles for decades, which included the following sentiment: "During Carl Jeppson's lifetime he was apt to say, 'We're not fooling ourselves, we know we can't take drinkers away from bourbon and rye blends, gin or vodka. Jeppson Malort is made for that small percentage of Americans who don't favor light, neutered spirits.'" (In a later version of the booklet, George updated the sentiment to "During the lifetime of our founder, Carl Jeppson was apt to say, 'My Malort is produced for that unique group of drinkers who disdain light flavor or neutral spirits.'")

Peter knew there was no chance such words came from the mouth of a Swedish immigrant. Even if they had—which they didn't—Carl Jeppson's audience wasn't a "unique group of drinkers who disdain light flavor or neutral spirits." It was his fellow Swedes.

In a black folder stuffed with marketing materials that sat on Pat's shelf was a copy of a *Chicago Sun-Times* article that also raised Peter's eyebrow. It was dated December 21, 1954—a year after George sold Red Horse Liquors and returned to practicing law. It was written by famed Chicago television host and newspaper columnist Irv Kupcinet, and a single curious sentence stood out: "Chicago businessman George Brode departs for Sweden next month to receive a decoration from King Gustav Adolf VI for his 20 years of promoting American-Swedish trade relations." George used the newspaper clipping for years to promote himself and Jeppson's Malört.

Pat knew nothing of the honor. Neither did George's kids. There were no keepsakes or mementos to suggest that such a trip happened or such an honor was bestowed. A visit to the king of Sweden might have happened—or maybe it didn't. It could easily have been a slice of imaginative George Brode marketing, and if it was, so might have been Carl Jeppson. Pat was clear that George never let the facts get in the way of a good story. To Peter, it seemed equally likely that Carl did or didn't exist.

Before meeting Pat, Peter spent hours digging through Swedish-language books looking for any evidence that Carl Jeppson or Jeppson's

Malört were part of a larger narrative. There were threads, but nothing
tied together. A single sentence from the one-page history Pat sent gave
him a springboard for his research: "Mr. Jeppson, a Swedish immigrant,
brought Jeppson's Malört to Red Horse and initially established the brand
by going from tavern to tavern (mainly along Clark Street) and offering
a taste of his product."

That, along with Pat's files and the memories he would wring from
their conversations, helped the narrative gel. He eventually found an
obituary for someone named Carl Jeppson that aligned with the time line.
There was no birthdate, but he died in January 1949, preceded in death
by his wife, Thekla. Still, Peter was skeptical. Nothing in the obituary
tied him to a wormwood liqueur.

The breakthrough came in a book by Swedish author and folklorist
Albert Sandklef called *Trettio Sorter Kryddat Brännvin* ("Thirty Varieties of
Spiced Spirits"), which made clear that Jeppson's Malört was no product
of George's creative mind. It had historical precedent.

Peter learned that Jeppson's Malört was in fact a kind of *besk brännvin*—"bitter liquor"—which was hugely popular in southern Sweden and
therefore would have appealed to Swedish immigrants in Chicago in the
late nineteenth and early twentieth centuries. The dots began connecting.

They connected further as Peter read about nineteenth-century
Sweden. Through the 1800s it was one of the poorest countries in
Europe and one of the last to industrialize. It was late to distilling, but
once it started, there was business to be had in spirits. As a new industry, the products were often wretched. Enter wormwood. It was among
the most powerful ingredients that masked flaws in the distillate. The
result, *besk* (or *bäsk*), became particularly popular in southern Sweden,
where Carl grew up.

Swedish emigration accelerated in the late 1860s, in the midst of a
two-year famine wrought by cold and drought. With options limited
and conditions dire, thousands of Swedes left the country every year.
Both Carl Jeppson and Malört made too much sense to have come from
George's imagination.

The revelation made Peter realize that Jeppson's Malört was a story of
Swedish immigration as much as it was a piece of Chicago history. As he

explored that history, Malört's place in it only made more sense. Swedes largely arrived in the late nineteenth and early twentieth centuries along the East Coast, most pushing west in pursuit of land. After landing in Chicago by railroad, many kept traveling north to the Upper Midwest. Plenty stayed in what was soon to become the nation's second-largest city, building culturally dense neighborhoods where Swedish was the language of the streets. By the 1880s Chicago had the second-most Swedes of any city in the world, a title it held until the 1960s.

After years of digging through newspapers, archives, and public records, the aha moment was finding Carl's grandson, Jim Jeppson, who was in his seventies and lived in suburban Dallas. He was stunned to hear from a guy in Chicago asking about his grandfather's brief run in the liquor business. Because yes, he was well acquainted with it. And yes, his grandfather was the guy behind Jeppson's Malört.

Peter would have loved talking with Jim's father, Gilbert, or especially his aunt, Martha, Jim Jeppson said. They knew all about it. He, unfortunately, didn't know much. And it was too bad Peter hadn't been in touch a decade sooner. When his father died, Jim found years of Malört ephemera strewn through Gilbert Jeppson's attic on Chicago's North Side—bottles, labels, photos, and more.

Peter held his breath and asked: Did he still have it? Any of it?

No, Jim Jeppson said. He threw it all away when his dad died.

Did he have *anything*, even one photo of his grandfather? Peter dearly wanted to memorialize the history of Jeppson's Malört with an image of Carl Jeppson. Just one.

Sorry, Jim said. All the photos were gone too.

A young Malört enthusiast's heart was broken. At least he had an answer. A Swedish immigrant named Carl Jeppson was indeed the source of Jeppson's Malört.

———————

Between public records, his budding understanding of Swedish history, and chats with Pat and Jim Jeppson, Peter pieced together what he could of Carl's life. It wasn't much, but it was more than there had been.

Carl Andres Jeppson was born in 1864 in Ystad, a picturesque town of cobblestone streets, quaint shops, and about five thousand people along Sweden's cool and rainy southern coast. As a young boy, he lived through the brutal national famine that sent immigration to the United States surging.

Carl moved to Chicago in 1888, at the age of twenty-four, landing in one of the city's dense Swedish neighborhoods, just north of downtown. He launched a small cigar manufacturing business, a common foothold for newly arriving immigrants.

In 1896 Carl married a fellow Swede, Thekla Samuelson, who was one year younger and came to the United States one year before her husband. Within a year they had a daughter, Martha, named for Carl's mother. A son, Gilbert, followed four years later.

Carl is believed to have run his cigar business until the 1920s, when he took a job, in his late fifties, as a railroad clerk. Gilbert also worked for the railroad; Peter's best guess was that the son secured a job for his father.

There was no way to know when Carl began dabbling with a home-made version of besk brännvin, but the 1920s, in the teeth of Prohibition, made the most sense. Peter combed archives of Chicago's Swedish newspapers but could find nothing about Carl Jeppson or his besk. He was left to guess.

What seemed likely was the story passed down through George Brode, that Carl walked the neighborhoods dense with Swedes—nearly 66,000 immigrants and more than 140,000 children of immigrants—selling the familiar spirit from back home, door to door. It was entirely plausible; Carl's generation of Swedes not only was familiar with besk brännvin and acclimated to its taste, but also wholly believed in its medicinal properties. Carl's side business may even have been legal. A loophole in the Volstead Act, the underpinning of Prohibition from 1919 until 1933, allowed medicinal spirits to be produced provided they were "unfit for beverage purposes." If anyone questioned Carl as he traveled Clark Street, he could always offer a taste of his intensely bitter besk. Surely no one would drink the stuff recreationally.

Peter and Chris began a standing monthly meeting at Pat's condo, the young men showing up on a Saturday morning with a bag of bagels and tub of cream cheese.

The three of them sat for hours, plotting a future for Jeppson's Malört. Chris tried exploring it as a brand, not just a name or a logo or even a product, but something customers perceived that elicited feeling and emotion. Disney equated to magic and Coca-Cola to refreshment—what was Malört? It was too abstract an idea for Pat. She just shrugged, though in the coming weeks, she eagerly reported coming across an article that made it click.

Chris's priority was building a website packed with historical information from the boxes on Pat's shelves, plus selling Malört T-shirts and posters from George's old marketing materials. Pat wasn't sure of the need, especially if they couldn't sell Malört online, which, for legal reasons, they couldn't. Chris explained the internet was far enough along in 2011 that most companies had a website; it was a modern tool for growing reach and, yes, building a brand. And certainly, he said, it shouldn't be left to some anonymous fan, as had happened with the social media accounts.

Peter's interest was in sharing Malört's history with the world. He also wanted to protect it. He suggested trademarking whatever they could—labels, terms, even the word *Malört*. That sounded complicated and expensive to Pat.

By noon at most of their Saturday meetings, Pat was drinking tall glasses of white wine while Peter and Chris tasted years of Malört that Pat had stashed in a dining room cabinet, bottles going back to the Mar-Salle years. It largely tasted the same to Chris, but Peter could spot the nuances: more bitter, less bitter, more herbaceous, drier, sweeter.

Every month, Pat shared a bit more about the history of Malört, at least as much as she knew. She talked about George and how she came to own the company. Peter took notes. He and Chris wondered why George left the company to his secretary, but they never pushed the question. Pat never said she and George were more than secretary and boss—but she implied just enough for Peter and Chris to surmise.

Peter was especially thankful for whatever happened between Pat and George. Without it Malört almost certainly wouldn't have survived.

George loved Malört and Pat clearly loved George—which made her care for Malört. She couldn't understand why anyone drank it, and it barely provided a salary, but more than once she said she kept it afloat mostly to honor George.

For Peter, that always led to the same question: Why? What did George see in Malört? Why did he care about some arcane Swedish spirit?

He asked Pat again and again, and every time, she shrugged and said George saw Malört as a challenge. Simple as that. It was his hobby. It was something to do. It made life more interesting.

For the first time in years, and really since George died, Pat was hopeful about Malört's future—as well as her own. Ten years earlier, she prepared for a career in medical transcription (though she never quite felt the need to follow through). Five years after that, thujone could have been her company's undoing. Now there was a path forward, and by the end of 2011, the news was good: Pat sold 1,959 cases, not much for most liquor brands, but for Jeppson's Malört, the most since 1994.

Back then the figure was a descending rung in a decades-long drop. Now it was a sign of hope—a nearly 50 percent leap from the year before, and nearly double the low-water mark of 2008. Pat wasn't sure a corner had been turned, but it was impossible to argue things weren't better.

She finally realized there was something bigger afoot, a cultural shift that included small-scale distilleries opening in the city and suburbs. It started in 2004 with North Shore Distillery, Illinois's first distillery in decades, launched by a married couple in a north suburban industrial park. KOVAL Distillery followed on the North Side of Chicago in 2008, also started by a married couple. A trademark lawyer opened FEW Spirits in Evanston in 2011, a mile from the Northwestern campus where George Brode attended college. By the end of the year came yet another Chicago distillery: Letherbee, founded by a rock musician and self-described "whiskey-drinking hippie" whose distilling career began with passing out his homemade moonshine at concerts.

In October 2011 the *Chicago Sun-Times* noticed the trend:

13

SAM

THE ENVELOPE CAME back to Sam Mechling marked DECEASED.

Inside were a letter and a check. The check, dated March 7, 2012, was made out to Pat Gabelick. Sam's compact, swooping signature sat in the lower right corner.

Sam wrote the letter on a typewriter bought at an estate sale around the corner from his apartment; he was the rare thirty-year-old to appreciate the snap of keys on paper, the way every letter mattered. He folded the letter twice before sliding it into an envelope and dropping it in a mailbox. It read:

> Dear Pat,
>
> Enclosed, please find a check written in the amount of $200. Your product has given me countless hours of joy over the years and has been a constant fixture in my circle of friends and fellow bar men. It has been the spirit of every celebration and the anesthetic of every defeat. It is our ally and our mascot. We love it.
>
> Please accept this check as a thank you for allowing me to make Malort such a huge part of my life and spreading the word about this wonderful stuff.

Three days later, the letter and the check were back in Sam's hands. How sad, he thought. Pat Gabelick was dead.

Pat Gabelick was not dead. She sat in her condo, not even a mile and a half from Sam's apartment, trying to understand why someone was profiting off her brand by selling unauthorized Malört T-shirts. Yet again, the source of the news was Mike Sula.

Just after the letter and check came back to him, Sam messaged the *Chicago Reader* food and drink reporter through Facebook, wondering if Pat was indeed deceased, as the post office seemed to think. It would have explained why he hadn't been sued, or at least why no one objected to him operating the Jeppson's Malört social media accounts. If she was dead, Sam wondered, who was running his beloved Malört?

If anyone knew, it would be the guy who wrote the most definitive Malört article to date. Sula didn't think she died—but to be sure, he called her on a Thursday morning.

Sure enough, Pat answered. Sula relayed details of Sam's message: after operating Malört's Twitter and Facebook accounts for more than a year, Sam started selling Malört T-shirts. He was a one-man guerilla marketing operation for her company. Pat scrawled hasty, confused notes, scarcely able to believe what she was hearing:

> Sam Mechling
>
> Facebook message
>
> Sent check
>
> Returned
>
> Deceased
>
> Holds contests with T-shirts
>
> Facebook—2,300
>
> Jeppson's Malort
>
> 1,000 Twitter
>
> Flicker—Malort Face
>
> Over a year
>
> Ohio

Sam Mechling arrived in Chicago in 2005, a fresh college graduate from the hills of northeastern Ohio. He majored in mass communications, minored in film, and figured he could do both in Chicago, a standard first stop for a young Midwesterner chasing big city dreams.

Sam grew up outside Youngstown, an Ohio steelworking town that was the bluest of blue collar, less than a hundred miles from both Pittsburgh and Cleveland. The Mechlings were not blue collar; Sam's dad was a local TV sportscaster who later went into money management. As a kid Sam watched his dad on the late news, then curled up on the floor outside his bedroom to await his return.

Chicago was the only place Sam wanted to be after college. He'd visited his sister there and knew he was built for the city—the people, the energy, the newness around every corner. Youngstown didn't have that.

Like many postcollege arrivals, Sam juggled hobbies and jobs. He worked on indie films and studied comedy writing at Second City. He always had a restaurant or bar job. He was a big guy, six feet two and 220 pounds, which made him a natural for checking IDs and breaking up the occasional fight. He shaved his head after starting to bald, which gave him an extra layer of menace. In reality Sam was anything but menacing; he was smart and funny and his high school pursuits genteel by Rust Belt standards: golf and marching band.

One night in 2005, after closing at a wine bar, a fellow doorman named Jason told him about a liquor Sam had never heard of. It was notoriously terrible, Jason said, available only in Chicago. He described it as tasting like cheap vodka swirled in a junk drawer, the one in virtually every kitchen, with a handful of rubber bands, a few pennies, and a couple of batteries.

Sam was intrigued. He'd developed an appreciation for strange and unpalatable things, finding value where many others didn't: David Lynch movies, old cars, weathered houses, vintage furniture—anything quirky or that had fallen out of style, all the better if scratched or dented.

He credited his father. When Sam was thirteen, Steve Mechling insisted his son join him restoring an old family farmhouse in the country, built in 1816, nearly three hours from Youngstown.

It seemed like pointless grunt work for a teenager, and Sam reminded his father at every opportunity.

"Don't look so sad," his father told him as Sam hauled a stack of photo albums. "This is heritage."

"Heritage sucks," Sam said.

By the time Sam lived in Chicago, heritage was cool.

In his new home, Sam wanted to become an old soul as quickly as he could. He soaked up the history, reading books and squeezing knowledge from old-timers, including a grizzled old newspaper reporter who spent hours at the wine bar telling his war stories.

Sam walked the streets, watching the neighborhoods bleed into each other, marveling how a single stoplight could shift the balance between languages, cultures, and smells wafting from the restaurants. To rest his feet, he'd grab a stool at a neighborhood bar, chatting up the bartender just short of becoming annoying. The good ones were some of the city's most informed and colorful storytellers.

Sam and Jason walked a mile from the wine bar to one of their go-to postwork spots, L&L Tavern. It was one of the city's legendary dive bars with a particularly dark lore, the sort that made Chicago riveting for a new arrival. Known as the "creepiest bar in the USA"—in part because of a hand-scrawled sign in the window touting itself as such—L&L was reputedly frequented by serial killers John Wayne Gacy and Jeffrey Dahmer. Gacy, who performed at children's birthday parties, supposedly visited at least once in full clown regalia; Dahmer, who killed more than a dozen men in his Milwaukee apartment, is believed to have sat in the L&L window, nursing a drink and watching the young skaters congregate in the Dunkin' Donuts parking lot across the street. L&L Tavern was also one of the city's most reliable Jeppson's Malört accounts.

As soon as they stepped inside, Jason steered Sam to the bar.

"This guy has never had a shot of Malört," Jason told the bartender.

A slow smile crossed her face, wry enough for Sam to know he wasn't about to taste something good. No one got that look when they were sharing something good.

The bartender grabbed the bottle and poured a shot. Sam sucked it down. Bitterness and astringency washed through him. It tasted like something that shouldn't exist.

Sam moaned, shook his head, and said the first thing that came to mind: it was like baby aspirin wrapped in grapefruit, bound with rubber bands, and soaked in cheap gin. Everyone laughed.

Sam grabbed the bottle and squinted at the label. He spun it around, looking for any clues about what he just tasted. There wasn't much, other than an extraneous apostrophe:

JEPPSON MALORT
Has the aroma and full-bodied
flavor of an unusual botanical.
It's bitter taste is savored by
two-fisted drinkers.

Bottled by
MID-WEST DISTILLERS PRODUCTS
Auburndale, FL

The bitterness sat on his tongue like an anvil. Sam swelled with emotion: bafflement, rage, lust, wonder. What *was* this? Why did it exist? And why the hell was it made in Florida?

He was worried he'd never find this weird thing again and offered the bartender twenty dollars for the bottle.

"Don't worry," she said. "You can buy the stuff."

The next morning Sam beelined to the liquor store two blocks from his apartment as soon as it opened. Sure enough, Jeppson's Malört sat on a quiet shelf, far from the whiskeys, gins, and vodkas that ruled the day. He carried the bottle home and opened it immediately, just to be sure it was everything he remembered from the night before. He poured a tiny shot and sucked it down. It was terrible.

He closed his eyes and exhaled.

"Thank God," he said.

What Sam tasted in Jeppson's Malört didn't make sense to most people. His friends and coworkers drank Irish whiskey and light lager, maybe a shot of Jägermeister for fun. The most adventurous drank craft beer and cocktails—things that made sense and tasted good. That was not Jeppson's Malört. Which was why Sam liked it.

In Malört Sam tasted a punchline. He tasted a tool to entertain and a weapon to wield. He tasted a conversation starter and a friend maker. He tasted bonding. He tasted heritage. Whose heritage, he didn't know, but he was desperate to find out. Above all he tasted opportunity. He knew he wanted Jeppson's Malört to be part of his life.

Sam eventually got a new job, at a bar a block from his apartment, one of the city's countless dim neighborhood joints christened with an Irish surname that filled with young, single professionals after work and on weekends.

The bar's owner thought Malört lacked any redeeming value, and he had no interest in carrying it. But he wasn't around much, and so long as the register was right, he asked few questions. So Sam went rogue. He bought bottles of Malört at the nearby liquor store and hauled them in for every shift, alongside a meal and change of clothes.

Circumventing a liquor distributor was illegal and could mean a fine of $1,000 or more. Sam felt he had no choice. He believed not carrying Malört was Chicago barroom malpractice. He kept the bottle out of sight, down with the well gin, vodka, and whiskey. It wasn't simply that he liked Malört and wanted other people to try it. It was that Malört made him the bartender he wanted to be: knowing, wise, and telling the city's best inside joke.

Sam poured shots for regulars. He poured shots for tourists—especially the tourists. No visit to Chicago was complete without one of these, Sam said, sliding a couple ounces of the yellow-green elixir across the bar. He'd tell them to pull out their phones and get ready to snap photos of their friends as the shots went down.

On slow nights he'd pour Malört for someone sitting at the bar to start a conversation. On busy nights he'd use it to shoo away an obnoxious customer demanding a free drink. He almost never charged for it. He poured it in the spirit of being an authentic Chicago neighborhood bartender. In the spirit of hospitality and conviviality.

One time Sam offered a shot to a man who couldn't hear or speak. The man sucked it down, winced, and then signed to his friend: "Why does this exist?" More than one woman pledged to break up with her boyfriend after being prodded into a shot. A bar regular, an Irish guy, sputtered after his first taste, "It tastes like a hobo's Band-Aid!"

What Sam loved most about Malört was that no one ever tasted it, shrugged, and got on with their day. Malört made poets of regular people. There was always a reaction, often followed by questions, the same things Sam asked at L&L: What was that? Why does that exist? A few people, also like Sam at L&L, couldn't shake their disbelief and wouldn't stop asking questions: Why does it taste like that? People actually like to drink this? It's only available in Chicago? It's made in . . . Florida?

Truth was, Sam didn't know most of the answers. There was no Jeppson's Malört website. He found the Flickr page, but that was clearly just some fans goofing around. There were no proper social media accounts speaking for the brand and sadly little media coverage. He searched *Malört* on the internet and learned it was Swedish for "wormwood." Then he looked up *wormwood* and learned about absinthe. His five-second explanation for customers became three pronged: Malört had the same bittering ingredient as absinthe, it was historically used by Swedes as a home remedy, and it could only be found in Chicago. That was about as much as he knew.

Sam ascended from doorman to bartender to bar manager. To boost business he turned to one of the most popular motifs of modern middle-class bar-going: a weekly trivia night, augmented with a little stand-up comedy from Sam himself. He loved to perform, to elicit response, and he'd push any button to do it. Then he realized the ultimate button-pusher was already there behind the bar.

To warm up the crowd, he'd pour a small shot of Malört for everyone in the room, then pass out blank cards. He'd take the microphone and instruct the audience to take the shot, then write down a description of what they just tasted, or a slogan for it. He'd give examples of previous winners, then give them the length of a song to come up with answers. The reactions, of course, were priceless. Then he'd flip through the cards and pick three winners.

The winners got some modest prize—a ten-dollar gift card to the bar, a T-shirt, maybe branded beer glassware. The real payoffs were the roars as Sam read through the cards aloud.

> Malört: Tonight's the night you fight your dad
> Drink Malört, it's easier than telling people you have nothing to live for
> Malört: Remind yourself why you stopped drinking

Trivia and Malört became the busiest night of the week. Sam eventually printed a flyer that claimed Jeppson's Malört as a sponsor of trivia night. It was part fantasy, part joke.

Sam kept the cards at his apartment, and slowly the pile grew. They felt like a stack of gold waiting for a second act.

Hungover on his couch one morning in September 2010, he was struck by an idea: if Jeppson's Malört still didn't have social media accounts, that meant they were there for the taking. He already had the content. He picked up his phone and, sure enough, @JeppsonsMalort sat there in the Twitter wilderness, unclaimed. Sam made a snap decision: *he* would be the voice of Malört. He felt the rush of knowing he was doing something he shouldn't—but that felt so right.

A day later he saw a handful of people marveling that *finally* Jeppson's Malört was on Twitter. Within a few days, Sam had a few hundred followers. Days later he crossed a thousand.

Sam took the swift popularity as license to follow his whims. People loved what Jeppson's Malört had to say; he was a foul, edgy voice for a foul, edgy drink, incorporating four-letter words few corporate accounts would dare. Sam offered no clue of the satire or that it was all one big joke. He played it straight to operate within a central tenet of comedy: laugh at your own jokes, and the jokes aren't funny. People therefore assumed the account truly did speak for Jeppson's Malört—why wouldn't they?

Sam had no idea what would happen. He didn't know who ran the company, whether there was a marketing team or high-priced lawyers to stop him. He just went for it.

A year later he also got the Jeppson's Malört Facebook account. He didn't start it—that was a woman even earlier to Malört than he was. Katherine Raz moved to Chicago in 1998 from Grand Rapids, Michigan, to attend Columbia College, a downtown school packed with artsy students.

Raz tried Malört for the first time in 2002, coincidentally enough, at the same bar where Sam discovered it—L&L Tavern. It became a running gag with her group of college friends. One of them described it as "pepper, then basement," a quote that followed Malört in their circle for years to come. Katherine thought it tasted more like furniture polish on a dusty dresser—though in a good way. She was initially scared to try it based on the reactions around her, but when she did, she was shocked that she liked it. It wasn't hot with booze like a shot of whiskey or tequila, and it had an interesting herbal character mingling with the intense bitterness. She drank it often. On a whim in October 2008, Raz made a Facebook page in its honor. It was done purely as a gag, and after posting a few times, she didn't do much more with it. Other Malört fans found it, though, and began posting, including Sam, who became one of its most faithful contributors. As Katherine lost interest to take on other projects, Sam reached out to ask if he could take over administrative duties. Raz didn't mind at all.

Sam quickly turned to the same foul-mouthed, edgy voice he used on Twitter. Among his first posts was a joke about a Malört cocktail named for Chicago's notoriously sharp-elbowed and foul-mouthed mayor, Rahm Emanuel: six ounces of Malört "poured into a swear jar and stirred with your right middle finger"—a reference to the mayor missing a digit he lost following an accident involving a meat slicer as a teenager.

When Jack Kevorkian, champion of assisted suicide, died in 2011, Sam posted a photo of the silver-haired doctor beside the machine that facilitated his patients' deaths. One of the three tubes led to a photoshopped bottle of Malört. The caption beside it read: "Son of a bitch! THAT'S how he did it! There goes the 'humanity' argument."

Sam launched a Twitter slogan contest with the winner getting a two-hour all-you-can-drink party at the bar where he worked. The winner was a slogan that would follow the brand for years to come: "Malört: Kick your mouth in the balls." Second place became even more legendary: "Malört: These pants won't shit themselves." A generation earlier, George taunted his audience by positioning Malört as a hallmark of masculinity. Sam did something similar—more gender neutral but still reveling in Malört's status as a brash outsider for masochists. Months after taking over the Facebook page, it crossed fifteen hundred fans. A few months later, it shot past two thousand. Sam became the internet's institutional voice of Malört.

His dad eventually told him that for all the promotion he gave Malört, he ought to get something for himself. Every week Sam introduced dozens of people to it at the bar and spoke to thousands on social media. Sam thought it sounded like a good idea—though he misunderstood the advice.

Steve Mechling, as dads will do, meant that his son ought to get a job working for Jeppson's Malört. Sam's creative and enterprising mind, as men in their twenties will do, heard something else entirely. So in February 2012 Sam decided to give Chicago what it wanted, and what seemed unlikely ever to happen otherwise: Malört T-shirts.

Sam had decent enough graphic design skills to transform Malört's red-and-blue crest into a digital image, pixel by pixel, above the words "Jeppson's Malört liqueur." Then he put in an order for fifty cotton T-shirts. Simple as that. The people working at the T-shirt shop were Malört fans and asked if Sam worked for the company. No, he said. They didn't ask any more questions.

Next Sam needed a website to sell the T-shirts. He sat down at his computer and tried buying the most obvious landing spot for Malört T-shirts: Jeppsonsmalort.com. It wasn't available. Strange, he thought.

The social media handles were there for the taking. Why wasn't the URL also available?

He settled on Malortchicago.com, then announced the sale February 16, 2012, on his Malört Twitter and Facebook accounts. All the shirts were black and straight cut, and they cost sixteen dollars. (Charging any more seemed to violate Malört's renegade spirit.) At the bottom of the webpage, he referred "all idiotic questions" to an email address he created for the enterprise. It was far from a high-tech operation and maybe even a dubious place to enter credit card information. But where else was Chicago going to get Malört T-shirts?

The next morning Sam knew Malört had the power to change his life. As he slept, the shirts sold out. When only small sizes remained, beefy guys still snapped them up just to have one.

Sam ordered another run. Those also sold out. By the third run, he felt emboldened to offer different colors and cuts for women. Within weeks he made a couple thousand bucks—just as his dad recommended, even if it wasn't quite how Steve Mechling meant the advice. Sam's parents were impressed at their son's diligence and industry, but also worried he might be setting himself up for trouble.

Sam was glad to have the money, but it wasn't what drove him. So he did what felt like the right thing, making out a check to Pat Gabelick for 10 percent of the profits. He typed a letter thanking her for allowing Malört to be part of his life, though he chose not to reveal details of his business operation; if she didn't know he was doing it, he didn't want to make her aware. If she did know, well, he didn't want to implicate himself. Really he just wanted to say thanks.

Little did he know, the internet turned up her old address, the apartment she left fifteen years earlier to take care of George.

Anyone who wanted to find the guy selling Malört T-shirts knew where to look. Sam didn't hide it. Paddy Long's was the place.

It was a newer entry to the Chicago bar scene, reflective of the shifting city. For seventy years, it had been Lawry's Tavern, a neighborhood joint known for its fried fish and cheap beer. In 2007, after a hasty makeover, it was reborn as Paddy Long's, geared toward the free-spending young- sters taking over the neighborhood, with a heavy emphasis on the city's booming craft beer scene. Sam started working there in summer 2010, living in the two-bedroom apartment above with a roommate. The first round of T-shirts was available only for pickup at the bar.

When Pat and Peter learned of the Malört T-shirt sale, Peter suggested he swing by Paddy Long's and learn what he could. No bluster, no sharp elbows—he wouldn't even reveal an affiliation with the brand. He'd just wander in and find what he could.

What he found was an affable, friendly bartender. Sam was chatty and pleased to meet Peter. Even after seven years in Chicago, Sam remained fascinated by the city's history, always hungry to know more—and Peter knew plenty. He had generations of history and knowledge; he pointed to the health club across the street and said his grandmother did gym- nastics there as a girl.

He told Sam stories about where the dead were buried from the Great Chicago Fire of 1871. He detailed the history of the Streeterville neighborhood, where Captain George Wellington Streeter's schooner ran aground in 1886, leading Streeter to claim the land as his own and build an army of followers to defend it. Eventually Peter pivoted to why he was there. A friend told him there were Malört T-shirts for sale. He was a fan, he said, and he wanted to buy one. Sam gladly obliged.

A few days later, Peter returned. This time he told Sam exactly why he was there. Sam flushed with jealousy—*This guy gets to work for Jeppson's Malört?!* It was Sam's dream job. Peter said he was there on behalf of its owner, Pat Gabelick.

"So she knows about the shirts?" Sam asked.

"Oh yeah," Peter said. "And she'll be coming to see you soon."

14

I HOPE HE IS
WATCHING US

BILL O'DONAGHUE STRODE down Diversey Avenue on a Thursday afternoon, flanked by Pat and Peter, ready to end Sam Mechling's fledgling career as Malört's number one fan.

Who was Sam to think he could operate Twitter and Facebook accounts on behalf of a brand he had nothing to do with? To sell T-shirts? To reap hundreds or thousands of dollars on Malört's name? A letter demanding he cease and desist sat in the briefcase swinging from Bill's hand. If necessary, Bill would slide it across the table and put a swift end to it all.

For years Pat never needed the kind of liquor attorney large companies maintained in droves, the ones focused on competition and regulation and the basic mechanics of operating a business. She worked simply and comfortably, the way George showed her, and she only ever needed a tax attorney. The wormwood issue flared up, and a high-priced firm in Washington, DC, dealt with it. She did anything she could to avoid a similar experience. Those things put Pat in a frenzy.

Rogue T-shirts made her realize she could no longer dodge the realities of running her business. Jeppson's Malört had grown increasingly complicated—more complicated than she liked—and she needed someone to help navigate the terrain. Bill O'Donaghue was the first attorney she talked to, and she liked him enough that she didn't talk to the other two names recommended to her. She found him in the most Chicago of ways: Peter, still working for the Chicago Cubs as a fan ambassador, met a well-connected bar owner in the Wrigley Field bleachers who happened to be an ardent Malört fan. Peter explained he was helping the owner of Carl Jeppson Co. and said she might need legal guidance. The bar owner offered three names, Bill O'Donaghue among them.

Sure enough, Bill knew his stuff, and in a frank and personable sort of way that put Pat at ease. He seemed to know everyone, and everyone seemed to know him. Pat trusted him immediately and hired him within days of learning of Sam Mechling's existence.

Bill was indeed as connected as they came in Illinois alcohol law, a former chairman of Chicago's License Appeal Commission, which considered appeals from businesses whose liquor licenses were suspended or revoked. He was also chief counsel of the Illinois Liquor Control Commission before returning to private practice in 2010. Less than two years later, Pat Gabelick called him. She was far from the typical client.

Not only was Pat's business impossibly small at fifteen hundred cases per year—"like a flea pissing in Lake Michigan," Bill liked to say—no other client was a seventy-year-old woman operating a liquor company on her own. He was charmed by Pat and her circumstances. He'd be out socializing and someone would start talking about Malört; Bill had the thrill of saying he represented the company. Fascination inevitably followed, especially when he talked about Pat.

Sam presented Bill with an immediate problem to solve. The rogue social media accounts, the vulgarity, the illicit T-shirt sales—it was all too much. Just a couple of weeks earlier on Facebook and Twitter, Sam shared what was supposed to be a joke about *Mad Men*'s Don Draper drinking Jeppson's Malört and committing sexual assault. As good as Sam was at building an audience, he could just as easily alienate it with humor that veered juvenile and offensive. The accounts were as much a space for his own performance as they were about building the brand— and that had to stop. Bill was optimistic that Sam was at least willing to meet; someone with questionable intentions would likely have ducked them or hidden behind a lawyer.

Sam's strongest advocate heading into the meeting was Chris Depa.

Through his digital marketing lens, Chris argued that regardless of whether he meant to, Sam made himself indispensable to the business. Jeppson's Malört had momentum among young Chicago drinkers, and it was Sam who gave voice to the momentum. He sometimes went too far—Chris saved a copy of the *Mad Men* post as an example of what couldn't be tolerated—but Sam did something no one else on the team could. Malört fans engaged with his content daily. Sam would need to be monitored and perhaps controlled, but the way he spoke to the audience he'd built was crucial.

Peter finally relented; from his couple of meetings with Sam at Paddy Long's, he detected sincere enthusiasm for the brand. Bill insisted he was ready for a fight if necessary. Pat was the least sure; she had no idea how she'd be able to trust Sam. Everyone agreed, though, that a conversation could be productive. If nothing else, they'd figure out his angle and gauge his sincerity.

Sam spied them the moment they walked into the bar, Bill in a suit and Pat dressed for a business meeting rather than an afternoon beer. Peter walked in behind them. They took a table in the back of the room.

Sam offered the trio something to drink. If they accepted, he thought, it might be a friendly conversation. If they passed, they were all business. They passed. He still figured he stood a chance. If they planned to shut him down, they could have done that with a letter. Instead, here they were, on his turf.

Bill did most of the talking as Sam nodded solemnly.

"You know how this could be viewed?" Bill said.

"Yes, sir," Sam replied.

"And you know we can stop this whole thing right here, right now, and it would be bad news in terms of your relationship with this company," Bill said.

Sam nodded.

"When were you going to pay us?" Bill asked.

Sam brightened.

"I tried," he said.

The check. Upstairs.

He sprinted to his apartment and grabbed the envelope marked Deceased. He ran back down and handed it across the table to Pat. There it was: the $200 check made out in her name, dated two months earlier. Pat passed the envelope around the table. Everyone laughed. Whatever tension that had walked in the door with them evaporated.

Sam sensed an opening, and he spoke quickly and excitedly, turning the moment into a job interview. He said he had about twenty T-shirts left, and he planned to share those profits with Pat too. He wanted to pitch Comedy Central on an internet sports-themed comedy show. He wanted to cultivate sponsorship deals to get Malört in front of the right people and grow its reach.

Sam struck Pat as charming and at least vaguely honorable. Like Peter, he was clearly part of the new generation that loved Malört. She shot Bill a glance that said there was no need for hardball.

Pat said she'd have that drink now.

———————

Instead of the cease and desist, Bill gave Sam a different document, a Transfer and Assignment Agreement—fourteen articles of legalese binding Sam to transfer his years of work on behalf of Jeppson's Malört to Pat, including the website, the social media accounts, and anything bearing the words *Carl, Jeppson's,* or *Malört.*

They agreed he would remain involved with the company as its social media director, and though he would have expenses reimbursed as Peter did, he would not draw a salary. He was free to pursue the Comedy Central and sponsorship ideas, but nothing was to be consummated without Pat's approval. All ideas were to be submitted in writing.

To show his newfound commitment to operating within the rules, Sam suggested in his first email to the team that Jeppson's Malört implement "a mandate of 'standards and practices' that Peter and I will strictly adhere to on a day to day basis" for the social media channels.

> I think this would be useful because Peter and I would be
> able to respond promptly to social phenomena with new
> material, jokes and pictures without having to bother you
> with 10 emails a day. In my experience, the topical stuff
> is by far the most popular. People LOVE it. That said, we

would maintain full accountability for the items that we post, and any deviation would be subject to reprimand or removal from the position.

It was ambitious talk from the guy operating Malört's social media existence as an outlaw just a few weeks earlier. It sounded fine to Pat. She didn't really care and didn't want to be bothered with the minutiae of social media posts. She had bigger concerns developing.

By the spring of 2012 she had assembled a dream team, albeit by accident: Peter, with a sense of Malört's history and a long-term vision; Chris, with his ability to bring the vision to life on the internet; and Sam, Malört's internet voice. But it all felt so rushed.

A year earlier she operated Jeppson's Malört quietly and alone and just as George did, as she had since George's death. Now she was surrounded by help, and help came with needs. Help wanted things—money, approval, more and more for her company. She had another lawyer to pay.

Pat remained wary of Sam. He charmed her more than she expected, but she wondered if they'd gone too easy on him. She warned Peter to be cautious; Sam was "a wheeler-dealer," she said. He had something to offer and he did it for free, but he'd never be more than that to the company, she said.

And Peter—he was so enthusiastic and ambitious and brimming with ideas, ideas at least a step, if not two, beyond the edge of Pat's comfort. His research showed him not only that Jeppson's Malört was a style of besk, but also that there was precedent for variations: versions less bitter, infused with flavor (he knew of a tasty Swedish brand accented with orange and cinnamon), and who knew what else was possible by manipulating how the wormwood was used and how long it steeped. It wasn't likely to happen at Florida Distillers, but one day, he told Pat, if she wanted to grow the business, it could be done.

Most of all, and most bewildering to Pat, Peter was determined to trademark decades of Carl Jeppson Company intellectual property—words, phrases, names, artwork, and, above all, the word *Malört*. Pat told Peter that his ideas, even simply building a website, had "gone way beyond where I ever imagined as far as costs go."

The world moved fast in 2012. Surprises came daily. They could be tiny or titanic, small as an unexpected envelope in Pat's mailbox or colossal as Brad Bolt, of Bar DeVille, inking a Malört tattoo on his left elbow.

A Malört tattoo! Pat could barely believe it.

Malört grew so entrenched in the Chicago zeitgeist that any small development earned media coverage, and so it was for the tattoo, at the Chicagoist website ("The Man with the Malort Tattoo"). As Brad explained to the reporter: "My first tattoo was the Chicago flag and I really didn't give much thought to ever getting more. Fast forward eight years and now my arms are covered almost completely. I wasn't happy with that first tattoo and I covered it up but wanted a different version of the flag. I decided on the crest and flag from Malört. I personally love the stuff and this version of the flag is perfectly in line with my profession."

Pat sent Brad a note on Jeppson's letterhead saying she hoped to see the tattoo, but between his late schedule and her early bedtime, it was unlikely to happen soon.

Meanwhile, an envelope arrived in Pat's mailbox that May, from someone named Patrick O'Neil, who lived on Chicago's North Side. Pat sliced it open and withdrew three neatly folded pages. The first was a letter:

> Pat Gabelick,
> Some experiences stay with you. The impact is immediate
> and expands on contact. Sensations and the idea linger,
> soon recede, then resurface in unexpected moments. Some
> who partake will return to the well again and again. Others
> will abstain but relive it in the intense instant of memory.
> So goes Malort.

On it went for several more paragraphs. Patrick first tasted Malört in 2008—a moment of discovery for a new wave of early adopters—at a performance at the legendary Second City comedy club. A bottle was sent through the audience, generating the predictable gasps and moans. Patrick was intrigued. A few days later, he bought the lone dusty bottle at his local liquor store. The clerk seemed stunned as he put it on the counter; the only person who ever bought the stuff was a lone older woman. She was the sole reason they stocked it.

A few years later, Patrick told Pat, he was clearing out papers and came upon "the enclosed versified verbiage. I would simply say poem, but given the nature of the spirit, hyperbole is in order, if not involuntary."

He titled the versified verbiage "Cruel Worm."

Malort
a rhythmic beckoning
for the tongue to cavort
in pungent and resurgent puckerports

Mellifractiously bitter
Carmel colored liqueur exhorts
crossing the taste buds
in perverse and lingering retorts

So says,
Malort

Down the gullet,
a flavor seedily supreme
sending skin shivers down the arms
eliciting olfactory screams

Oh, who can abide?
Who can deny
its insistent hint
of shag rug's unseemly underside?
And a finish most unforgivably, unforgettably,
oh so bontaniacally snide?

Eyes moisten
Nose flares
Mind reels and jigs

Yet, here I am taking another swig
and muse to no one,
Do I still have hair or am I wearing a wig?

Amid dizzying gastrointestinal strife,

Malort
a little less
Malort
a little more
Ah, such is life

Time passes, crinkles, and lunges

Just as the gullet forgives to forgets
Malort surges from the gums.
With a sudden panic I wonder,
Do I still have opposable thumbs?

Malort

This liquid most maniacally peptic
Has also made my mind dyslexic
Raising a glass, glistening and short
I rasp to the bartender, "Another . . ."

Lamort

Pat replied to Patrick via the email address enclosed: "I am awed by your words and so grateful that you chose to share them with me." She clipped the pages together and stuck them in a file she labeled "Malort Poem."

Malört inspiring tattoos? And poems?

What was happening?

Word was spreading. Jeppson's Malört was no longer just a Chicago story.

In spring 2012, two media outlets with massive, albeit vastly different national audiences, the *Onion* and the *Wall Street Journal*, reached out. Pat couldn't believe the interest—the *Journal* especially. It was George's favorite newspaper, read daily front to back.

Whatever skepticism she couldn't shake about Malört's rising fortunes finally blew away in a single moment on a warm Tuesday evening in late May 2012. It was Malört's first public event.

Peter suggested the idea weeks earlier. Pat thought it sounded strange. *An event? For Malört? Why would anyone come to that?*

What Peter knew and she still didn't was the importance of connecting with an audience in the era of "craft" and "local" drinking. A generation earlier, alcoholic brands existed facelessly and ubiquitously, made in far-off factories and replicated as generic experiences coast to coast. Now it was about beer festivals. Whiskey tastings. Brewery tours. Cocktail classes. Beer-pairing dinners. The new generation didn't simply want brands—it wanted experiences.

The result was called the "1st Annual Malört Night!," featuring three-dollar Malört shots and five-dollar Malört cocktails—face-twisting versions of margaritas, mojitos, and Manhattans made with Malört. On social media, the team touted the chance to "meet Malört employees for the first time!" and to "talk to a real Malört historian!" (One Facebook reply said it was "great to know that this will be spectacular and awful at the same time!") The location, Nisei Lounge, two blocks from Wrigley Field, was one of the city's best Malört accounts.

Pat fretted like a nervous party host—*What if no one comes?* Sure enough, as the 6:30 PM start time loomed, turnout looked slight. Peter and Sam were there, of course. Bill O'Donaghue came. The *Wall Street Journal* reporter showed up to take notes and shoot video.

Pat, dressed in black pants and a short-sleeved aqua turtleneck—she favored turtlenecks because they covered scars from her burns—sat at the bar drinking white wine, figuring she was right all along. No one really cared much about Jeppson's Malört. Peter's exuberance got the best of him.

She chatted with Bill, her back to the door, and when she turned around, she saw something remarkable: a room full of people. An extra-alarm fire at a furniture store along the city's El tracks had halted trains for nearly three hours, which slowed everyone's arrival. But there they were. Ready to revel in Malört. The room suddenly felt electric.

As bartenders poured shots and shook cocktails beneath Christmas lights strung across the ceiling, Peter stood before the crowd and introduced himself as "the Malört historian." He was dressed in a white-collared shirt tucked into jeans, nearly shaking with adrenaline, thrilled to be talking to a room of strangers about this thing he loved.

He said he got involved with the company out of sheer curiosity, wanting to learn more about Malört and maybe chronicle its history because there wasn't much online. He talked of digging through Pat's files and the decades of history he discovered. He briefly explained what he'd stitched together: Jeppson's Malört was an old Swedish drink sold by a man named Carl Jeppson. Carl came to Chicago from Sweden's southern coast. Peter talked of George buying the company after Prohibition and being honored by the king of Sweden—which got a roar of laughter and applause.

Peter spoke for ten minutes, then took questions. First up: What ingredients make Malört taste the way it does?

"I'm not going to give away our recipe," Peter said. "But suffice to say, the name Jeppson's Malört—"

From the crowd came a cry: "Baby tears!"

Peter understood the shock aspect of Malört. It got people in the door, both literally and figuratively—it no doubt helped pack Nisei Lounge and accounted for much of the enthusiasm in the room. He also wanted people to appreciate its history as he did. He knew it would be a process. So he rolled with it.

"Baby tears, yes," he said.

He paused, then continued: "The main ingredient in Malört, I'll just put it this way, the name of the drink is Jeppson's Malört, and Malört is the Swedish word for 'wormwood.' I can't say anything more than that, but maybe if I'm drunk, I'll tell you later."

Everyone laughed.

After a few more questions, someone asked, "Is Malört sold in other cities other than Chicago?"

Peter repeated the question before delivering an emphatic answer.

"No," he boomed. "Malört is only sold in Chicago."

It was the loudest applause of the night.

At the end of his presentation, Peter summoned Pat to join him. She nervously clasped her hands as he introduced her to a roar of cheers. Sam also joined, wearing one of his black Malört T-shirts; Peter introduced him as "our Twitter fellow." Pat couldn't believe the response, doubly bewildered as starstruck youngsters asked to pose with her for selfies afterward.

It was a magical and heartening evening with a single regret. As Pat told the *Journal* reporter, she wished George could have seen what became of his lifelong hobby.

"I hope he is watching us," she said.

Two weeks later, after months of work, Chris Depa clicked the Jeppson's Malört website to life. Behind an image of a man slumped over on a stoop after what seems like a hard night of drinking, it said:

> Welcome Jeppson's fans. We've just come out of our Malört-induced coma and we're getting ready to unload years of repressed Jeppson's angst on Chicago!

Below sat a photo of the team, snapped at Paddy Long's, a smile on every face and a shot of Malört in hand: Peter, Pat, Sam, and Chris. Pat got the honor of holding a bottle of Malört.

The company finally, officially, had a lifeline to the world, operating as something more than an oddity lurking on back bars and the dustiest store shelves. There was a link to buy T-shirts and the company's first point-of-sale marketing material since George's heyday decades earlier: Jeppson's Malört table tents that Chris designed for bar managers to print and perch throughout their establishments. Pat also wanted to devote a page to Patrick O'Neil's poem.

From left: Peter Strom, Pat Gabelick, Sam Mechling, and Chris Depa, taken at Paddy Long's in 2012 for the first Jeppson's Malört website, which launched that year. *Courtesy of Chris Depa*

There was even an email address: a Gmail account Peter made a couple months earlier. (Pat had trouble accessing the Gmail account and wanted to forward incoming mail to her personal AOL address. Chris advised against it: "If patrons get email responses from an AOL account, Jeppson's Malört will be the laughing stock of Chicago. . . . Details like that matter, and it's a much bigger deal than you think.")

There was no sign of the *Journal* article, but *RedEye*, the *Chicago Tribune*'s free daily tabloid targeting the young, free-spending, bar-going commuters core to the rise of Jeppson's Malört, ran a cover story in August with a headline that wrote itself: Worst Shot in Chicago?

The morning it published, Sam posted a photo on Facebook and, as was his way, prodded Malört fans by suggesting they were unhoused: "I know most of you guys use The *Red Eye* as a blanket, but you just might wanna save this one." It more than doubled the engagement of Malört's previously most popular post. As hundreds of reactions streamed in via shares, likes, and comments, Sam emailed Pat: "People are excited."

So was Pat—though she was also bewildered. Beyond media coverage, demand was clear in the monthly sales, which barreled toward 3,233 cases sold in 2012—the most since the high-water mark of 1973.

The success felt increasingly complicated. Malört was around so long, and as such an afterthought, it fell through the cracks of modern alcohol distribution as the rare brand represented by competing distributors in the same territory: the smaller, scrappier Stoller Imports, which had dozens of oddball labels that made Jeppson's Malört a natural fit; and Wirtz Beverage, a behemoth with some of the biggest brands in liquor, including Jack Daniel's, Captain Morgan, and Tito's Handmade Vodka.

For years both Stoller and Wirtz ordered the minimum seventy cases every month or, in the leanest years, seventy cases every couple months. In late 2011, just about the time Peter Strom began telling Pat the currents might be shifting for Malört, the strangest thing happened: Wirtz doubled its order. The next month it did so again. And then again. By the middle of 2012, Wirtz reliably ordered 140 cases a month. Stoller still sold less but also started asking for more.

Both companies amped up the pressure, squeezing Pat for additional cases she didn't have. In May 2012 she used the interest to raise the price for the first time in eight years, from $84.75 for a twelve-bottle case to $90. If sales trends held up, it would equate to an additional $20,000 a year in revenue, a boon to the bottom line after decades of decline.

It did little to quell demand. The battle between distributors grew fiercer. Wirtz called Pat to complain about its customers jumping to Stoller. Stoller called Pat to complain about the price increase. Pat had no idea how to navigate any of it.

She appealed to veteran bar owners she met through Peter for guidance, admitting she was at a literal loss for words during hard conversations with distributors. She told one of the bar owners she was "extremely naive" and knew how to operate Jeppson's Malört only when it was scraping by. She had no idea how to navigate demand.

Finally, Pat faced a decision. If Malört really was surging into the mainstream, consolidating momentum made sense. Her growing network of industry insiders largely advocated that she go all in with Wirtz. It was the obvious choice, accounting for about two-thirds of sales. Someone from Wirtz had casually suggested a few years earlier that Pat cut Stoller out. Pat worried that depending on one distributor would make her beholden—what if Wirtz then decided not to prioritize Jeppson's Malört?

She'd be stuck. Now that she had everyone's interest, aligning with one distributor made more sense.

In late summer 2012 she made the move, to the chagrin of Stoller salespeople who had championed the brand as an underground Chicago staple for years. But it was an obvious call. Sam had built a voice for Malört across social media; events and a website connected it to the world; now Wirtz promised to stomp on the accelerator. It immediately started ordering more than two hundred cases a month and slotted the brand in its craft spirits portfolio. It had no idea where else to put it.

With Pat fully on board, Wirtz asked her to address its salespeople at the company's monthly sales meeting—exactly what George did years earlier to drum up support and enthusiasm. It was a thrill for George, a relentless showman and advocate of his beloved hobby. For Pat, the thought of speaking to all those strangers turned her stomach. She had no choice but to agree, and she resolved to speak as little and as briefly as possible. She asked Peter, Chris, and Sam to help—both to write the presentation and to be by her side for it. They couldn't have been more eager.

Pat stocked her fridge with beer for hours of preparation and offered to make appetizers. And of course, there would be as much Malört as the guys wanted.

———————

They pieced together a presentation, each doing what they did best.

Pat would open with an introduction. Peter was to follow with Malört's history and a technical understanding of what exactly it was—and why it tasted like *that*. Sam would close with a few zingers and lead a tamer version of what he did in the bars—no f-words, he was told—leading the salespeople in a rollicking back-and-forth on how to talk about Malört's unique taste. (Chris didn't make it due to work.)

They stuffed one hundred envelopes with copies of the *RedEye* article and a short history of the brand. They set aside six bottles to pour samples for everyone in the room. Pat's contact at Wirtz told her to dress nicely, which she had already planned to do, but he motivated her to buy a pricey silk blazer at Nordstrom for the occasion.

By the morning of the presentation, all three were racked with nerves. Just before going on, Peter did a shot of Malört, a little to calm himself, a little to summon good luck. Pat, almost unheard of for her, did the same. Sam skipped the shot, scurrying off to a bathroom to handle a last-second bout of anxiety knotting his stomach. He was fine performing for a room of strangers. This was something else entirely. So much seemed to be on the line.

They were led down a hall that seemed to lead nowhere, then pushed through a door that placed them at the front of a spacious conference room lined with Wirtz's dozens of products. About eighty salespeople sat before them, silent and waiting. It felt like a call from the minor leagues of Pat's condominium to the majors.

Pat's heart raced, and she did what came naturally: she admitted how dreadfully nervous she was. The faces before her turned to a sea of reassuring smiles, and all at once she felt better. Then she began to read her notes, telling the story she'd increasingly told in recent months:

> Good morning.
> My name is Pat Gabelick and I am the owner of the oldest liquor brand in Chicago, Jeppson's Malört.
> I have been with the company for over forty-six years. In 1966, I was hired as a legal secretary by George Brode, the original owner. When he hired me, he didn't tell me that he owned a brand of liquor. I spent half my time on the job preparing legal documents and the other half stuffing envelopes, since there was no such thing as the internet at that time and George was a big believer in direct mail. We sent frequent letters to all our customers and all our salesmen, and in those days we had over thirty distributors. If any of you have been in liquor sales a long time, you may remember our letters. When George passed away in 1999, I took over the company.
> I am fortunate to be accompanied today by two young men, Peter Strom and Sam Mechling, who are working without benefit of salary. They came to me because they

love Jeppson's Malört and believe in the product. I would
like to think that you will come to feel the same way. With
your help we can continue to grow.

She introduced Peter, who shared a version of the presentation he
gave at Nisei Lounge: from Carl Jeppson's birth in southern Sweden to
George's efforts to sell Malört between the 1950s and his death in 1999.
After a decade of Pat running the brand, he said, the next milestone
came that very year, as Jeppson's Malört began its first social media push
and finally launched a website. Like Pat, Peter's nerves also faded as he
spoke; everyone seemed fascinated to hear what he had to say. For so
long Malört was an oddball mystery to most people in the room. Now
someone was giving them answers.

Finally, as one-ounce samples circulated through the crowd, Sam
came up for his usual good time, defaulting to his favorite description
of Malört as tasting "like baby aspirin wrapped in grapefruit, bound
with rubber bands and soaked in cheap gin." Pat followed with a round
of Malört trivia based on their presentations, handing out T-shirts for
correct answers.

It couldn't have gone any better. When they finished, Pat, Peter, and
Sam walked triumphantly to the back of the room to watch the next
presenter talk about some brand of bourbon. They felt bad that he had
to follow their act—like a poet following a punk band.

Pat grew anxious about the *Wall Street Journal* article, and for good
reason. By the end of June, the reporter, Mark Peters, emailed to let
her know it had been, as he described it, "shelved." He didn't offer an
explanation other than to say it was not uncommon as an article wound
through the editing process. He hoped to resuscitate it, "but there's no
guarantees," he said.

Pat was crushed. She nursed dreams of Peter proudly, maybe even a
touch smugly, presenting the article to the liquor stores that laughed him
out the door in recent months when he suggested they carry Malört. For

weeks she checked in with Peters hoping for good news. He was on to politics and natural disasters.

Pat told her lawyer that such setbacks made it hard to believe a turn-around was truly at hand: "Everyone seems to have such high hopes for Jeppson's Malört. I sure wish I was not a glass half empty person. It does not seem possible to me."

What she didn't know was that Peters was equally disappointed—and determined to get her story in print. He'd chipped away at the article for months after discovering Malört at an office going-away party, fascinated not only by its taste but also by the fact it was unique to Chicago, and somehow with Swedish roots. When Peters found out who owned the brand, he was only more intrigued. He spent several hours interviewing Pat, by phone and at her apartment, amused by her swirl of bafflement and excitement at Malört's seemingly rising fortunes.

He saw the profile as an obvious fit for the *Journal*'s A-hed column, a daily front-page staple since 1941 that explored subjects surprising, funny, and, ideally, a touch absurd. Fierce competition among hundreds of *Journal* reporters made landing an A-hed arduous, requiring layers of approval. Peters got his editor in Chicago on board, but the bigwigs in New York weren't so sure. It was a funny story—but funny enough? It was an obscure subject—but obscure enough? Peters saw plenty of arti-cles die in process over the years, but this time the prospect particularly bugged him. He knew he had a great story.

It sat in the system for months, largely forgotten and not quite fin-ished. Then came the holidays, when reporters headed off for vacation and editors became desperate for copy. Peters saw his opportunity. He convinced a New York editor to read it over. The editor said it lacked one thing: Peters needed to stretch beyond Malört diehards to find an anecdote of someone taking a first sip. He found it at High Dive, a neigh-borhood bar on Chicago Avenue, a few blocks from Bar DeVille, where a man downed a shot, winced, muttered an expletive, and said Malort's "awfulness is throwing me for a loop." That got Peters over the goal line.

Two days before Thanksgiving, it finally happened, and when it did, Pat was dumbstruck. Front page. Of the largest and most influential news-paper in America. The one George read faithfully every day for decades.

Below the headline IN CHICAGO, A SPIRIT RISES DESPITE BITTER REVIEWS, Peters wrote of Malört's "growing following among Chicagoans as a kind of badge of honor. A shot of it is a way to punish a drinking buddy or out-of-towner."

A bartender said it had become "the shot of choice" for people working in the bar and restaurant industries. Another bartender said it had transcended that niche to find a more mainstream audience, "from an inside joke to something people are seeking out." Pat, for the world to see, didn't hide her disdain of her own product:

> Ms. Gabelick seems a bit baffled by the interest in Malört, which was a hobby for her boss, George Brode, a Chicago lawyer who left the company and its one product to her when he died in 1999.
>
> "All my life I wish George had made a product I could drink," she says.

Pat heard from all corners of her life after the *Journal* article finally ran. Even George's son David, whom Pat hadn't talked to since the estate closed more than ten years earlier, called to congratulate her. She called Peters, choking up as she thanked him, saying how proud George would have been.

More than eighty years in the making, it was finally clear, and even George Brode wouldn't have seen it coming. Jeppson's Malört was a cultural sensation.

15

WHAT IF WE MADE OUR OWN MALÖRT?

THE 2012 RESURGENCE of Jeppson's Malört came in many forms. Peter Strom's growing authority. Sam Mechling's arrival. Bringing on Bill O'Donaghue to navigate the complexities. A website. T-shirts. Consolidating distributors. Surging sales. A media blitz that included more than eighty articles mentioning Malört; in 2011 there were twelve. As Pat entertained ever more questions from ever more reporters, George was often on her mind.

"He would have loved this," she told one interviewer. "He would have loved to be doing this interview with you instead of me. He liked to talk to people. So, I'm doing it in his memory—in his honor."

With the increased attention came more events. The first, at Nisei Lounge, went well enough that the team hosted a few more before the end of the year. One was at the legendary Murphy's Bleachers, just beyond Wrigley Field's outfield wall, where Sam and his comedy act were incorporated for the first time. Another was at Brixie's, the west suburban bar whose longtime fascination with Malört had bartenders mixing it into cocktails—usually poorly—since at least 2009. A finely dressed Cook County criminal court judge showed up, saying he was a longtime fan. Pat was always curious who drank Malört; that it could be such an esteemed member of society amazed her.

At Paddy Long's, where Sam worked, they hosted a Malört-and-cheap-beer fest: three-dollar Malört shots and an array of lowbrow regional beers. It was Sam's idea, figuring the two were a natural fit—odd, old things rediscovered by hip, modern audiences.

Pat couldn't help but fret ahead of each event, just as she had before the one at Nisei. *What if no one comes? What if the chatter is so loud that the audience can't hear Peter and Sam?* There was always something to worry about, but she realized, yes, people really were interested. She also learned something she never knew about owning Malört. It could be fun. Really fun.

After a decade largely alone, Jeppson's Malört got her back in the bars for the first time in years. She forgot how much she loved it. She loved socializing there in her twenties, and it turned out that she loved socializing there in her seventies. Better still, in her seventies she was surrounded by people charmed and fascinated by her: *This is who owns Malört?!* It never made sense that people wanted to talk to her; she felt she hadn't earned the attention. But she liked talking to people, and it was easy. All she had to do was sit there and sip chardonnay, tell her stories, answer a few questions, and bask in the adulation.

Pat even learned to take the occasional shot of Malört with her admirers. She'd never tasted the stuff until she owned the company, but it finally came to seem like part of the job. Like taking medicine. People tried to ascribe Malört's sudden relevance to Pat, but she shrugged it off, even when younger women approached her in bars to say she was an inspiration.

"The bartenders liked it and the hipsters liked it, and it took off," she told one interviewer. "I didn't do a thing."

The truth was that by 2012, after a decade of operating Malört on autopilot, Pat *was* a savvier business owner. A bar owner suggested she send thank-you letters on Jeppson's letterhead to some of her most dedicated accounts. Pabst Brewing did something similar in the '90s, the bar owner said, and some bars still had the letters framed on their dingy walls. It made sense to Pat; you could never go wrong showing appreciation.

She borrowed liberally from the Pabst letter while writing to Nisei Lounge, the Green Mill, Bar DeVille, and Murphy's Bleachers. Sometimes she added her own personal touches or enclosed Jeppson's merchandise, usually a sweatshirt or a T-shirt. She wrote to Scott Martin at Simon's Tavern after meeting him one summer evening and listening to his stories of tasting Malört as a child and talking to George on the phone in the 1990s. She knew fewer and fewer people who remembered him, or who had even heard of him.

"One of the things I really enjoyed about your tavern is that it had a mix of old and young drinkers and they both seemed equally at home," Pat told Martin. "That's pretty rare these days."

The longtime customers, like Simon's, ordered ever more Malört. Bars that once had to be prodded into ordering now wanted to know how many cases they could get. And new customers kept coming. When Scofflaw opened in spring 2012 as Chicago's latest hip cocktail outpost, with a focus on gin, it did so with Malört on draft. On draft!

Every week staff twisted open a dozen bottles to refill the two-gallon keg beneath the bar. Neighborhood regulars guzzled it, especially with friends visiting from out of town, an increasingly common "here, you have to try this" ritual. In one swift year, Scofflaw became Malört's second-biggest account in the city, eclipsing even the Green Mill.

Word soon began spreading beyond Chicago. A Seattle wine and liquor store reached out to say it wanted to carry Malört and tried connecting Pat with a local distributor to make it happen. The idea fizzled away after a few emails, but Pat marveled at interest in Malört from two thousand miles away.

In New York City, Owen Gibler, a former Violet Hour bartender, stocked Jeppson's Malört at Mother's Ruin, one of Lower Manhattan's next-generation cocktail bars, either hauling bottles back from Chicago or having friends send them by mail. John Giovanazzi added Malört to his Los Angeles bar, Complex, in 2012 after tasting it in Chicago a few years earlier. It was an immediate hit with Chicago transplants or Chicagoans passing through, especially bands playing his stage. He built an entire "rare spirits" section stocked with brands unavailable anywhere else in Los Angeles. Nothing else generated the fanfare of Malört.

In July a film shooting in Chicago called *Drinking Buddies*, a story of tangled twentysomething relationships set in Chicago's beer industry, asked for Malört to sign off on product placement. Pat agreed, which led to a legendary Malört description reaching the silver screen: "Like swallowing a burnt condom full of gas."

In November food and drink raconteur Anthony Bourdain tasted Malört for his television show *The Layover,* saying its brash nature created "a possibility that I could get all stabby and belligerent."

By the end of the year, Wirtz Beverage began plotting an obvious and low-risk next step: heading across the border to Wisconsin. Other than brief distribution in Wisconsin in the 1970s, it would mark the first time Malört would be available beyond Chicago. If ever there was a moment for growth, this was it.

So yes, by 2012 things were going well. So well that after decades in the wilderness, Jeppson's Malört not only found its place in the culture—it also inspired an imitator.

———————

The idea struck Robby Haynes over shots and beer at Whirlaway Lounge, a seventy-year-old Chicago dive bar in the midst of a trendy resurgence, much like the Logan Square neighborhood around it.

Robby, bearded with a dark mop of hair, managed the bar program at the Violet Hour. He sat with Nathan Ozug, who worked at Letherbee, one of Chicago's handful of small, upstart craft distilleries. Once entirely the domain of large companies with exacting processes and sprawling warehouses, distilling was in the early days of a small-scale revolution by entrepreneurs with shoestring budgets who believed they, too, could make bourbon, rum, gin—or maybe even the strangest of all Chicago spirits.

Robby turned to Nate.

"What if we made our own Malört?" he said.

Like most everyone in Chicago bar circles, Robby heard of Malört long before tasting it. It was dreadful, he was told. Horrifying. Comically bitter.

Robby's first taste finally came as many did: someone handed him a shot in a bar after work. It left him anything but horrified. Malört's towering lore had him braced for something so bitter, so intensely foreign, that he wouldn't be able to stand another sip. Instead, he found its inter-section of arch bitterness and herbal heft strangely pleasant.

A few years earlier, he would have had no idea what to make of Malört. Robby's first job after moving to Chicago from North Carolina to make music was as a valet at a dance club. His hustle got him noticed, and he was brought inside to haul ice, stock bottles, and wash glasses as a barback. He took to the work, parlaying it into a similar job at the Violet Hour.

Just as the Violet Hour gave a steak-and-martini city a fresh appreci-ation for classic cocktails, Robby gained an appreciation too. He mixed bitters, sliced endless citrus, built house-made syrups, and found a taste for imported spirits, especially Cynar, an earthy-sweet Italian aperitif, and Chartreuse, the shimmering green French liqueur. Both were bold, herbal flavors that made Malört make sense. Though Malört was far too jagged for the earliest incarnations of Chicago's most exclusive cocktail list, even that eventually changed.

In 2011, Malört's earliest days of surging into the city's consciousness, it finally appeared in a Violet Hour cocktail. Toby Maloney encouraged his bartenders to challenge him with new ideas for the bar's quarterly menu updates. Andrew Mackey, who managed the bitters program, surprised and amused Toby by suggesting what he called the Wicker Park Sour. Before tasting it, Mackey was told Malört was reminiscent of "a burning Band-Aid at the bottom of a dumpster." He eventually realized it could work in a cock-tail if layered properly. The Wicker Park Sour included an ounce of Malört plus several ingredients to soften it, including simple syrup, honey syrup, grapefruit juice, and egg white. Toby waved it through to the menu, which finally put Malört behind the Violet Hour's bar. It only took three years.

By the time he sat at Whirlaway, Robby had worked his way from barback to bar manager. The job included weekly meetings with the owners, some of the biggest industry names in town. Every week he was asked: "What can we do to stay ahead?" Robby cast about endlessly for inspiration, hoping to show up at one of those meetings with *the idea* that would open eyes around the table.

At Whirlaway Lounge, he had it: *What if we made our own Malört?*

The details followed quickly: a version more layered and nuanced than Jeppson's, and a recipe that turned the single bracing, bitter note into a narrative across the palate. It was so obvious that Robby couldn't believe he hadn't thought of it sooner. If anything, he wanted people to take Malört more seriously. The jokes and marketing around Malört face were fun, but he knew its heritage stretched across an ocean and generations, long predating the Chicago bartenders who found it in late-night bars.

Robby began sketching the recipe on the back of a cocktail napkin.

Grapefruit pith and grapefruit peel were a must. They would lend a bright citrus note only implied in Jeppson's. Elderflower would offer a soft, floral counterpoint. Traditional alpine herbs would round it out: fragrant star anise, bitter gentian, and piney juniper. Its core, of course, would spin around the same essential axis as Jeppson's: wormwood.

Robby started playing with the idea at the Violet Hour the next day, before doors opened, using the same tools that had blended countless cocktails. He eventually came up with a decent enough approximation of Jeppson's Malört to begin appearing in Violet Hour cocktails.

Grander visions followed. Robby called Brenton Engel, owner of Letherbee Distillers, the self-described "whiskey-drinking hippie" who proudly touted he was "free from corporate compromises" and beholden to "absolutely zero influence from outside investors or marketers."

Engel agreed to scale up the concoction, exclusively for the Violet Hour. They tweaked the recipe for the bigger batches, adding honey to make it sweeter and more palatable before deciding they'd made it *too* palatable. Eventually they found the balance: all the bitter-herbal-citrus character of Jeppson's Malört, rounded into something silkier.

The first run of cases landed at the Violet Hour that fall, adorned with a crude black-and-white drawing of a cloaked, crowned king strumming a harp. And there it was: Robby's vision brought to life, an idea lying dormant in his brain, waiting for a few shots and beers at Whirlaway Lounge to be knocked loose.

––––––––––

The conquest was announced on October 12, 2012, in, of all places, the *New York Times*.

The original label for
R. Franklin's Original
Recipe Malört, which
was initially available
only at the Violet Hour
cocktail bar in Chicago.
Courtesy of Robby Haynes

Beneath the headline ANOTHER TASTE OF MALÖRT IS ARRIVING IN
CHICAGO, a veteran reporter of the cocktails, bars, and spirits scenes
opened with obvious context ("The wormwood liqueur's flavor is so
intensely bitter and sharp, you probably thought you had somehow
offended the bartender, and he or she was now exacting revenge")
before breaking the news that Jeppson's Malört had competition from
"an in-house expression of Malört," forged as a collaboration between
Letherbee and the Violet Hour.

Robby explained that his version was a reaction to disappointment
in the original.

"The first time I tasted Malört five years ago, I didn't find it unpleasant, but I thought 'Wow, what was that?' It was intense and bitter and floral and all these things," Robby told the *Times*. "Now, when I take a sip, I find it to be less remarkable. I don't know if my palate changed or what happened. I wanted to make something that lived up to what Malört was like in my head."

He called his interpretation "significantly more nuanced and layered."

"It has a beginning, a middle and an end," Robby told the *Times*. "It's not just flat—'Here's something that's bitter, but tapers off.'"

Ambitions were modest for his take on Malört, he said, little more than intriguing the modern wave of spirits and cocktails enthusiasts: "There's a small contingency of people that are into it. It's not intended to be for the masses."

They named it for Robby, employing his first initial and middle name: R. Franklin's Original Recipe Malört.

Of course they called it a Malört. What else would it be called?

———————

The rise of Jeppson's Malört wasn't without its challenges and hurdles, doubts, and insecurities. But it had been a thrill, an ascension beginning with Mike Sula dragging Pat from bar to bar in 2009, when she had her first inkling that, yes, people might actually care about her odd little product. Then Peter Strom's email landed in her inbox in 2011, followed by the unlikely boon of Sam Mechling commandeering Malört's internet voice—and then all the sales and media coverage and events that followed. To be discovered and to be adored, especially after decades of struggle—it was the stuff of dreams.

R. Franklin's Original Recipe Malört put an end to those sweet and innocent days.

It was the tiniest of brands, not even available for purchase at stores. Yet it was the first truly *holy shit* moment of Malört's rise, the moment Pat, Peter, Chris, and Sam knew they were no longer just a scrappy underdog story. They were bigger than they understood.

Pat had her team of industry insiders—bar owners on speed dial, her brand manager at Wirtz, Bill O'Donaghue—but she didn't know what to do other than to worry. This was so far from the playbook she learned under George.

Peter was apoplectic. For months he'd warned of the potential fallout from failing to protect Malört's intellectual property—especially trademarking the word *Malört*.

All along, Pat was skeptical. You couldn't trademark *vodka* or *gin*—those were styles of liquor, not brand names. How could you possibly trademark *Malört*? And why spend money on lawyers if it couldn't be done? Wasn't Jeppson's Malört in fact *a malört*?

Even Bill O'Donaghue agreed. He told Pat the odds of securing the trademark were slight.

Peter insisted. Based on his research, in both English and Swedish, he was convinced that Malört wasn't *a malört*—it was a besk. In Sweden, he said, comparable brands were all called besk. Malört—that is, wormwood—was an ingredient in the products, and a bottle of besk might say as much. It was never in the name.

Peter said he could get his former Swedish professor at North Park University to help build an iron-clad case. He admitted he didn't know the legal underpinning of what needed to happen next, but he was confident of his conclusion.

"A Swede would never name their product the way we have, because it wouldn't make any sense," he wrote. "Our use of the term Malort is now totally unique and refers only to our product."

Peter was equally frustrated by Pat's inaction and Bill's skepticism. In June—four months before the emergence of R. Franklin's Original Recipe Malört—he emailed Pat saying he "woke up in a cold sweat last night worrying about" the issue.

> I mean, Malört is the most important and unique word in our brand. If it's not trademarked or copyrighted or whatever it is we need to do to protect it, then other people can use it to make knock offs. I don't want that to happen, Pat.

> I'm sorry I'm so angry. I'm not mad at you. I've kinda
> put it outta my mind for awhile, but reading all this Swed-
> ish information on the Malört just brought it all up again
> and made me realize the absolute importance of getting
> Malort protected for the company.

A couple weeks later, he sent a detailed letter to Bill explaining why
he believed the word *Malört* could be trademarked. Bill, in the midst of
conducting his own research, was unswayed. In mid-July Pat conveyed
Bill's position to Peter: "He does not believe we can ever trademark the
word and that it is not worth spending the money trying."

Bill felt no need to discuss the subject with Peter—Pat was his client,
not this eager kid. Peter knew Bill didn't take him seriously, which only
exasperated him more. Finally, Peter gave up.

> If I could only have a few questions answered directly, learn
> more about all the legal options out there, I feel Bill and
> I might be able to figure something out. It feels like we're
> missing each other's point on this issue. I know that he's
> the lawyer and knows more about legal things, but after all
> this work, I just want to know why this is the case.
>
> That said, if Bill is right, our only option is to get the
> word out as fast and as often as possible that Besk is the
> name of the style and not Malort. Because we won't be
> able to do anything else.
>
> I'm sure you're sick of all this, so I'll let you go.

Four months later, R. Franklin's Original Recipe Malört arrived.

After nearly a century of barely surviving as an odd Chicago footnote,
times and tastes finally changed, so much so that the unthinkable happened: *two* versions of Malört. Soon there would be a third.

This time the idea came from John Laffler, co-owner of Off Color Brewing, as he visited Paul Hletko, who owned FEW Spirits, another of the Chicago area's upstart craft distillers. As much as he loved beer, John loved Chicago bar culture. He spent several nights a week at the Map Room, one of the first bars in the city to embrace a draft list of imports and the earliest craft beers. It also carried Jeppson's Malört.

John first tasted Malört at the Map Room and didn't much like it. He quickly came to appreciate it: the intensity, the bitterness, its rite-of-Chicago-passage nature. About once a week, the Map Room's social winds steered him toward a shot, and he eventually applied his brewer's palate to his appreciation, recognizing batch-to-batch variations in booziness, woodiness, sweetness, and of course bitterness.

Paul also knew Malört well. He was a musician turned trademark lawyer turned distillery owner, familiar with Malört from playing bar shows in the '90s and early 2000s. It was always on the back bar, always there as a cheap shot. It was still years from being fashionable. It was just there.

On this day John visited FEW to learn about distilling. At some point he floated an idea: their own version of Malört. There was, of course, Jeppson's. Robby's collaboration with Letherbee had come out a few months before. Why couldn't they make their own?

FEW mostly did whiskey, but there was no reason not to try a take on Malört. Paul and John did it right then. There was no wormwood handy, so they used orris root—less bitter and needing less sugar for balance. It couldn't quite be called delicate, but it was lighter and mingled more easily with other herbs and botanicals than Jeppson's Malört. Paul deliberately let it overmacerate to boost the bitterness.

In late 2013, a year after Robby's take on Jeppson's Malört, FEW released its version, a scant 150 bottles, a fun lark never intended to be repeated. It was named for the feeling of drinking such a thing—Anguish and Regret. Below that, in bold letters, read a simple description of the product: "Malört."

16

MOVE OVER, MALÖRT

PAT OWED R. Franklin's Original Recipe Malört a debt of sorts.

Despite her doubts, and Bill O'Donaghue's doubts, she had to go for it. It was time to ask the US Patent and Trademark Office (USPTO) for a trademark on the word *Malört*.

In January 2013 Pat grew the inner circle once again by hiring another lawyer, this one with thirty years of trademark experience, and watched the expenses mount. Peter urged applying for the trademark for months, but it likely wouldn't have happened without the feeling that there was no choice. Pat worried about wasting tens of thousands of dollars to learn that, in fact, she could not trademark *Malört*.

The new lawyer, Bill McGrath, was hopeful, though—and felt personally invested. He'd learned of Malört a few months earlier, during that fateful summer of 2012, as its reach and interest spread across Chicago. McGrath's adult children were hosting a backyard barbecue for friends at the family's northwest side Chicago home. A member of the group, known affectionately as Uncle Andy, brought a bottle of Jeppson's Malört, insisting it was made with weeds plucked from along the expressway running through Chicago. Malört faces unfurled in all directions. McGrath took a shot. It was a bitter punch in the face, but he found it curious and intriguing.

When he read about Letherbee's version that fall, his personal curiosity turned professional. It seemed like an issue ripe for his expertise.

He reached out to Bill O'Donaghue, who said that yes, in fact, they were interested in trademarking the term. Bill McGrath met with Pat, who agreed to hire him. He was thrilled to represent such an unlikely and iconic brand.

Pat sent him the company history Peter had stitched together, along with Peter's arguments for the trademark. Bill McGrath quickly concluded odds were good they would be able to trademark the word. He expected the Patent and Trademark Office to consider *Malört* a descriptive term, and descriptive terms typically could not be trademarked. But, he told Pat by email, "if a mark has acquired distinctiveness from long use and recognition as a trademark, the USPTO will allow registration due to the acquired distinctiveness." If Jeppson's Malört had anything on its side, it was distinctiveness and long use.

To support the case, Pat and a team of volunteers gathered affidavits from twenty-two current and former bartenders, including a few who sold Malört all the way back in the 1960s and '70s. They worked at some of Chicago's most recognizable bars—Nisei Lounge, the Green Mill, Nicks's Beer Garden, and Lincoln Tap Room—and affirmed in legally binding documents that a customer asking for Malört was understood to mean Jeppson's Malört.

Pat even drove an hour to the suburbs to get an affidavit signed by Tony Uzzardo, the longest-tenured Malört fan she knew. Tony, seventy-five at the time, had his first taste more than fifty years earlier, handed to him by his father, a second-shift factory worker who tended bar at the union hall after getting off work at 1:00 AM. He always started with a shot of Jeppson's Malört. George Uzzardo told his son Malört helped settle his stomach. It might taste bad, he said, but it made you feel good.

When Tony retired as a printing supervisor in 2001, he kept his father's tradition alive, downing a daily 4:00 PM shot in his kitchen. When he and his siblings visited their father's grave, they'd pour a little out for him—though Tony always insisted his father would have preferred they drink it.

When a batch tasted too sweet in 2003, Tony tracked down Pat's number to let her know. She apologized with two bottles she had in storage of the good old bitter stuff he remembered. They stayed in touch.

When she needed someone to affirm to the USPTO that *Malört* could only mean Jeppson's, she turned to Tony. He signed an affidavit attesting:

> I was introduced to Malört by my father when I was old enough. He always had a daily shot of Malört.
>
> I have introduced Malört to my immediate family, my extended family, and now my grown children.
>
> I now continue the family tradition of the daily shot of Malört.
>
> I recognize the name Malört as referring only to the Jeppson's Malört brand alcoholic beverage.

As the evidence grew, McGrath was even more optimistic about getting the trademark—though they wouldn't know for months. That left the question of what to do in the meantime about R. Franklin's Original Recipe Malört. They could sue, but Pat insisted she didn't have the money, and certainly not enough to sue every version of Malört that might follow. Her brand manager at Wirtz had a secondary concern about a lawsuit: suing a start-up distillery would be terrible public relations. David would become Goliath.

Yet they had to do something, as the coverage following the *New York Times* scoop showed. "Violet Hour Malört gives Jeppson's high-class competition," read the *Huffington Post*. "Thinking they can do better, hip Wicker Park bar the Violet Hour has created their own malort," wrote CBS. Said *RedEye*: "Move over Malort? Chicago bar to brew their own beast."

Pat wanted to move over for no one but played it cool when the *RedEye* reporter contacted her.

"If that's what they want to do, God bless them," she said.

Letherbee's take was a more approachable version, she noted, made with "all sorts of other flavors which we don't do."

"If they want to make it more palatable, I guess that's fine," Pat said. "But it certainly wouldn't be Malört."

Chris Depa bemoaned the press this new competitor was getting and wondered if it might be worth sending Letherbee a polite letter explaining that Malört was the brand name, not the style of liqueur. As long as it was available only at the Violet Hour, the situation wasn't so critical. But how long would that last?

"I would hate for them to decide to begin selling it outside of the Violet Hour . . . as Malort," he emailed her.

"There's nothing we can do," Pat replied.

Bill McGrath wasn't so sure. A week after filing for the trademark, he suggested trying to spook Letherbee with a cease and desist to show Jeppson's was intent on securing the copyright, though even that came with risk. If Letherbee ignored the letter, Pat would corner herself into suing. If she didn't, Bill O'Donaghue warned, her threats would be meaningless—"a paper tiger with no teeth." The word *Malört* would be lost forever.

Still, Bill O'Donaghue sent the letter, arguing that Jeppson's had "achieved a position in the alcohol beverage market place that is unique and distinctive," and the word therefore was its alone: "To say the average consumer would, when you mention Malört, only think of Jeppson's product would be an understatement."

He turned Robby's interview with the *New York Times* against him as proof of Letherbee's infringement.

> You are using the uniqueness, distinctiveness and popularity of Jeppson's Malört to promote your product. In fact in your press comments you specifically state that your product is an attempt to make a Malört similar to Jeppson's and invite consumers to assume that the two products are similar. Mr. Haynes is quoted in the New York Times Diner's Journal on 10/12/12, as stating, "The first time I tasted Malört five years ago . . . I wanted to make something that lived up to what Malört was like in my head." There can be no doubt that you are intentionally appropriating, using and imitating Malört for commercial purposes.

In response, they heard . . . nothing.

R. Franklin's Original Recipe Malört not only remained behind the Violet Hour bar, Letherbee did just as Chris feared, pushing into wider distribution in spring, packaged in a sleek, rectangular bottle with a trim blue label dominated by a single word in bold white letters: "Malört." After ignoring the cease and desist, the outsize use of the word *Malört* felt to Pat like an unmistakable slap.

So was what followed a month later, when the *Reader* named R. Franklin's "Best Locally Made Malört" in its annual "Best of Chicago" issue. Noting that Jeppson's Malört was made in Florida, R. Franklin's, the *Reader* said, was "truly local."

Most dive bars didn't care about R. Franklin's, but the hippest bars in Chicago and New York did, and they quickly began mixing it into cocktails, including the Violet Hour, which introduced the Thigh High— Letherbee Malört, gin, bitters, sweetened egg white, and orange flower water. It was novel enough for a *Chicago Tribune* reporter to review the cocktail, describing it as "an almost shockingly bitter punch upfront, but one that mellows with each sip."

Letherbee's Malört was roundly hailed as a successful and interesting update of Jeppson's. A *Chicago* magazine review described Jeppson's as

Once Robby Haynes and Letherbee Distillers scaled up R. Franklin's Original Recipe Malört for distribution in stores and bars, it was given a cleaner look fitting into Letherbee's portfolio. *Courtesy of Robby Haynes*

smelling like "rubbing alcohol" and tasting of "nail polish remover," its bitterness given a rating of four yucky faces. Letherbee's smelled of "herbaceous gin" and tasted like "bitter grapefruit," the magazine said. It was given a mere two-and-a-half yucky faces. The conclusion was inescapable: Jeppson's was Jeppson's. Someone might want to savor Letherbee's.

As the months dragged on, Letherbee continued ignoring the cease and desist. Bill O'Donaghue assumed it meant they didn't believe Pat had a claim to the word *Malört*, and they dared her to sue. Though she had the larger company, they calculated, correctly, that Pat didn't want the fight.

With no resolution in sight and still awaiting word from the US Patent and Trademark Office, triage was needed. Chris emailed Pat to warn her of the urgency: "We need to begin elevating our brand a bit so as to not alienate the upper class that they are aiming for."

Pat agreed, but she had no idea how to do it.

Chris had an idea: rein in Sam.

———

Sam talked a good game about cooperation and teamwork when coming on board as social media director. Chris advocated for him, saying only Sam could maintain the voice he'd built online. Eventually Chris convinced Peter. All they wanted was the momentum to build, and at the dawn of social media, Sam had mastered one approach. He connected Jeppson's Malört to its fans every day through the devices in their pockets.

Early on, Pat continued to insist Sam would never be part of her company. Bill O'Donaghue remained skeptical about him. Chris and Peter convinced them. They quickly regretted it.

It wasn't personal. None of it was. When Sam joined the team, Peter put any hesitation and misgivings aside and chose to start fresh, to give a chance to the guy who sold the T-shirts and posted sexual assault jokes. Sam was saying all the right things.

He just couldn't follow through. Sam rarely sought approval for his social media posts, and he continued to speak for Jeppson's Malört in the same sardonic voice. He posted a video to Facebook titled "What does

Malort taste like?" that showed a man taking a shot, followed by images of grapefruit and honey while a jaunty tune played. Then, reflecting Malört's impossibly long and bitter finish, the music abruptly shifted to the jarring cacophony of twentieth-century German composer Carl Orff as the images shifted to gasoline, ear wax, and Adolf Hitler holding a can of bug repellant. Enough eyebrows raised that Sam replaced the video with a tamer version, minus Hitler.

A month later came his most infamous work, the one that had Chicagoans rushing to see his showmanship in person. It was a twin billboard above a pizzeria at a busy intersection on Chicago's North Side. The first billboard showed a bottle of Woodbridge sparkling wine with two glasses. It read, YOUR WIFE JUST HAD TWINS. The second billboard, featuring a bottle of Malört, said, THEY WERE JOINED AT THE HEAD.

Curiosity seekers flocked for hours to the six-cornered intersection of Lincoln, Racine, and Diversey to see if Jeppson's Malört had really done it. Among them was Malört's rep at Wirtz Beverage, who pulled a swift U-turn after getting a call about the billboards on the way to his family's Indiana beach house with his toddler daughter in the backseat. He called Pat on the way.

"If Sam really did this, I'm gonna lose it," he said. "If he Photoshopped it—OK, you don't know what a Photoshop is, but we'll talk about it. In that case, it's genius."

It was indeed Photoshop. And it may have been genius. It was also a problem. Wirtz also distributed Woodbridge, and the rep had no interest in pitting two of his customers against each other. There was also the possibility of lawsuits—from Woodbridge, from the billboard company, and from the pizzeria below, Gino's East. Pat emailed her "boys," as she'd come to call them, with a warning.

"While I realize that you all love the Jeppson's Malört brand and enjoy working with the company, if you wish to continue working with me I would ask that you all try to think like businessmen," she said. "The picture that was posted on Facebook on Friday could cost me the company. Both Woodbridge and Gino's East could sue me. It needs to be removed immediately, but since it's already gone viral that isn't going to help the situation."

Thing was, Peter and Chris needed no convincing. They saw Sam's desire for short-term buzz directly opposed to their goal of long-term growth. If Jeppson's Malört was to be positioned for the future, ready to navigate a new wave of competitors, it couldn't rely on shock and buzz. As Chris told Pat by email:

> I really don't think Sam's sense of humor is really good for Jeppson's in the long run. Things like the Hitler video and the copyright infringements are lewd and unethical and most people aren't attracted to that. In order to continue expanding and attracting a following beyond what we now have, that kind of humor needs to be toned down and become more mainstream.

Chris proposed implementing a program that would require administrative approval—that is, from him or Peter—before Sam could post anything to Jeppson's Malört social media channels. He argued it was the plan when Sam came on board earlier in the year, before "we all got busy with other things, with life, and Sam kept doing his thing without our attention."

"It was all OK until it wasn't," Chris said.

Pat worried about Sam's reaction and wondered if simply asking him to tone things down would be enough. She said she didn't want to stifle his creativity.

Chris and Peter very much wanted to stifle Sam's creativity—or at least tame his impulses. If Sam wasn't on board, Chris said, there were countless people across Chicago who would be thrilled to run social media for Jeppson's Malört without the occasional lapse in judgment. With his bar industry expertise, Chris said, Sam was better than anyone on the team at coordinating events; maybe they could shift his attention there.

And then it happened again. Sam made another glib social media reference to sexual assault on April Fools' Day, announcing a series of neon-colored Malört wine coolers that included a flavor called "G-rape." Among the people to respond was a woman who emailed with the subject line "Rape jokes are not funny."

"I've been raped," she wrote. "Many women you know have been. None of us are laughing. Losing customers. Nice one."

Sam responded to her by saying the joke was "really aimed at the creeps who use wine coolers to get women drunk. . . . We despise this facet of drinking culture, and that's why we're making fun of it. So, please make an attempt to grasp that you can make a joke about rape without condoning or glorifying it."

The woman wrote back to say Sam should resign from the company. "Clearly not a man who is sensitive to the market," she said.

Sam first tried to minimize the outrage, telling Chris that the people complaining weren't "true Jeppson's fans. They're just extremists and militants." It didn't matter, Chris said. Some Malört fans might be amused by such humor, but plenty weren't. Just as important, the company needed to talk beyond its existing fans. It needed to speak to new fans.

The post was taken down before Pat could find it; she wasn't even sure what it said until Chris sent it to her the next day. He also recommended taking down the *Mad Men* post from the previous year. Pat said she assumed Chris already handled that. No, he said. He left social media to Sam—and Sam hadn't done it. As he had months earlier, Chris wondered if it was time for a change.

"I mean, this is not rocket science or a marketing issue," Chris told her. "It's an issue of common sense and integrity. If Sam doesn't have either of those qualities, then you need to consider the possibility that Sam isn't the man for the job."

A day later Sam told the team he thought an apology was in order and insisted he wasn't "interested in winning any debates, even though my views vary greatly from these individuals." Pat left it to Sam and Chris to decide whether to post the apology on the Jeppson's Malört social media channels or to email each person who complained individually. (Chris advised the latter, saying a public apology would only exacerbate backlash.)

It was against this backdrop that Carl Jeppson Co. awaited not only word on its trademark application but also a response from Letherbee to the cease and desist—grappling with its growing popularity while trying to secure its identity. If Pat lost the word *Malört*, what was left?

So when she asked Chris what she could do in response to Letherbee, he had an answer. He'd been saying it for months.

Rein in Sam.

The fact was, business was good. Really good. Never so good.

The heights of 2012 were on their way to being lapped by 2013, which shaped up to be the best year yet for Jeppson's Malört: more than four thousand cases sold. Since George began keeping records more than sixty years earlier, that never happened.

The growth likely would have come with or without Peter and Chris. The bartenders and "hipsters," as Pat called them, embraced Malört. A cultural shift was on. Peter and Chris *were* there though, and they'd been indispensable to steering her company into the twenty-first century. They helped it make sense.

But communication had become spotty. Resentments grew. Peter boiled over with ideas and dreams, arguably too many for someone not fully on the payroll. He wanted more responsibility, to be by Pat's side as she ran the company. He thought he'd earned it. He wanted to be on emails with Bill O'Donaghue about the trademark issue. He wanted to take the lead on licensing issues. Neither happened.

Frustration mounted. He called less, responded to fewer emails, and stopped coming around except with Chris to talk business. Optimism occasionally flickered and he'd reengage, apologizing for becoming "so intense," explaining he was "very passionate about helping you and this company succeed. I have never been a part of something this awesome." Then he'd drift away again.

By spring 2013 Pat emailed to express concern: "I want you to know that I care about you and am anxious to have the old Peter back. I know how much you love Jeppson's Malört, but do you need to take a year off and forget about us and concentrate on the rest of your life?"

She didn't hear back.

Meanwhile, Pat grew increasingly fond of Sam. Despite her initial doubts, he charmed and impressed her. She began going to Paddy Long's every Wednesday at noon, Sam's lone daytime shift. She sat at the bar chatting with him, sipping three glasses of chardonnay over a couple of hours—always three glasses—and buying shots of Malört for whoever accepted. One afternoon a barbershop quartet walked in and Pat bought them a round. They thanked her with a rendition of "Sweet Genevieve," which both delighted her and got her teary eyed; Genevieve was her mother's name. Paddy Long's became a weekly highlight of her social calendar.

Soon Sam started visiting her at the condo. She'd drink wine and he'd have a few Guinnesses. She loved drama—especially the more wine she had—and talking about her cat. Sam helped her pick out and install a new desktop computer and a new television, both game-changing for a single, seventy-year-old woman. When Pat had to take her cat to a vet appointment in a neighborhood with little street parking, Sam drove her.

Much as she used to do with Peter, Pat talked to Sam about life and love, the past and the future. When Sam got a new girlfriend, Pat was one of the first people he told. Pat gave smart advice and drew on her own experiences while coming of age in the '60s, like a cool aunt with tremendous war stories. She confided something she never told Peter and Chris: she and George were very much in love. They traveled often and had a wonderful life together. His death was very hard for her. Pat and Sam barely talked about Malört when he visited.

Pat and Sam in Pat's condo, 2013. *Courtesy of Pat Gabelick*

Pat also came to appreciate something about Sam that Peter and Chris couldn't. He just wasn't a process guy. He was a free and creative spirit whose ideas had to spin unfettered into the world. He was quick and clever and knew how to talk to people, how to make them laugh. He pushed boundaries and sometimes it worked. Sometimes it didn't. Sam's side gig as a stand-up comic impressed her. Getting up in front of a room full of strangers and making them laugh—it seemed so brave.

Pat was fond of Peter and Chris. She valued their friendship. They were the first connection she'd had to the new generation of young drinkers, and they helped move her company forward. She just connected more deeply with Sam. She thought he had a brilliant mind. He was edgier and funnier—though the misfires kept coming.

During the summer of 2013, in a post promoting a radler made with Malört, Sam made light of Chicago's chronic gun violence. Beside a photo of the radler, Sam wrote, "In a Chicago summer riddled with gunfire and open volcano-like heat, there is only one weapon that can save you . . ." The outrage was swift enough to garner coverage in *Crain's Chicago Business* ("Jeppson's Malort's Social Media Misfire"), which noted the company was typically "social media-savvy."

But if Pat was the cool aunt, Sam was the charming nephew. He filled a hole in Pat's life.

The shift in dynamics was clear within the operation. Peter led the first Malört event, at Nisei Lounge, in spring 2012. Sam had only officially been with the company for a few weeks, and he didn't say a word to the crowd. By fall Sam was leading the events. While planning an event in the suburbs, Sam arranged to tell jokes and lead one of his Malört slogan contests in the main bar on a PA system. Peter's historical presentation was relegated to the pool room "to an intimate audience, unamplified," Sam instructed the bar. That way, he said, "the people that want to hear it can, and the revelers can keep on reveling."

The company's identity was shifting, from Peter's dream of Malört taken seriously by modern audiences to Sam's party and punch line.

Chris dealt with the conflict head on. Jeppson's Malört was ultimately a job. A fun and interesting job—but a job. He treated Pat with the same professionalism as his clients. When there was conflict, he discussed it, evenly and dispassionately. His thoughts occasionally drifted to a future where Pat was ready to get serious, move production back to Chicago, open an office, and build a workforce—sales, marketing, communications—like any liquor company. If that happened, he could see a place for himself. If it didn't happen, no problem.

Malört was never just a job to Peter. As much as Sam, he *loved* it. Helping Pat was the intersection of his passions. And the momentum they'd built! When things got tough, his frustration became clear and it could boil over. Rather than talk things out, he withdrew.

Even as the brand continued reaching milestones—including finally expanding distribution to Wisconsin in the middle of 2013—Peter remained curiously silent as Sam, Chris, and Pat discussed how to share the news.

They worried that Chicago drinkers thought of Malört as theirs and theirs alone. Would they get blowback for growing? Pat said George briefly sold Malört in Wisconsin about thirty-five years earlier, which Sam suggested they use to their advantage. "We need to let them know that any feelings of betrayal are a misplaced, foregone conclusion and therefore not worth having," he wrote to the group. "We break the news and move on with confidence and enthusiasm."

Everyone was on board with the idea, but as was his way, Sam also wanted to lead with shock and awe: "NEW STATE, NEW VICTIMS," he told the group. Chris said he found the slogan "too self effacing" and that they should aim to "make our brand slightly more approachable." Even as Chris and Sam asked him to weigh in, Peter stayed silent.

Pat was left to talk with Chris, who said he also hadn't heard much from Peter lately. He said Peter may have withdrawn because he no longer saw where his involvement with Jeppson's Malört was headed. Peter was also in the midst of breaking up with a longtime girlfriend, which didn't help.

Chris confided that Peter was frustrated with Sam—and so was he. He acknowledged Sam was talented and said he hoped they could continue

The most "unforgettable" liquor on the planet...

Now available in WISCONSIN.

WIRTZ BEVERAGE WISCONSIN

A postcard touting Malört's entry into Wisconsin in 2013 after decades of being sold only in Chicago. *Courtesy of Pat Gabelick*

working together, but his general approach to the job—"Sam acts first and asks forgiveness later"—was "counterproductive to what Peter and I are trying to do for you and it seems like every time we take one step forward, Sam propels us three steps back."

Then he gave his first indication of where things might be headed: "If more constraints aren't put on, then it might just be too frustrating to work with him." The implication was clear: *it's us or him.*

Pat confided the growing power play to Sam. Just as Chris had said months earlier that there would be no shortage of people to replace Sam, Sam now suggested the same of Chris. "He has a great eye and perspective, but it's a big world out there and working for a company like yours is a draw of immeasurable strength," he said. "People will fall all over themselves to work with us."

In May Jeppson's Malört finally began distributing in Wisconsin. Pat, Sam, and Peter reprised their presentation from the previous year for the distributors in Chicago. Pat noticed this group seemed more relaxed and casual, though she was still petrified.

It was invigorating for the team to do something new, to cross borders and introduce Malört to a new audience. It was exactly what Peter and Chris wanted for the brand. After that trip, they decided there might be one more chance to make it all work. They resolved to write a business plan charting a future for Jeppson's Malört.

Nearly six months had passed without word from Letherbee when Sam, dressed in a Malört T-shirt on a warm June afternoon, browsed the stalls and galleries lining the annual Milwaukee Avenue Arts Festival. Two guys approached him.

"Do you work for Malört?" they asked.

Yes, Sam said. He was always proud to say that.

They introduced themselves as Nathan and Ian. They worked for Letherbee. Nathan was sitting at the bar when Robby was struck with the idea that led to the months of discord.

The meeting was brief but cordial enough. Nathan and Ian said they were concerned about the legal tangle between the parties and hoped it could be resolved.

Sam relayed the encounter to Pat, suggesting they follow up without lawyers to reach a conclusion. The lawyers, of course, opposed the idea, but Sam and Pat went ahead anyway. Sam sent an email to Brenton Engel, who owned Letherbee, to play the role of good cop, saying he wanted to "speak to you as a peer."

"My message is serious, make no question about that, but I hope you understand that it is motivated by professional courtesy, respect, and admiration," Sam wrote. "I want to help."

Carl Jeppson Co. was about to sue Letherbee, he said: "Simply put, this is not going away, and we're running out of time." However, he said, he could get the company's lawyers to stand down long enough to work out a tidier solution.

They got their first response from Letherbee in six months. Robby replied, saying they were curious about the possibility of a "peaceful resolution."

Yet the issue ground on. Pat endlessly crunched the numbers, by hand on a small white legal pad, tallying her legal expenses and fretting that a blinking contest might undo her company. In September she calculated fees eclipsing $45,000—more than her salary in recent years. Sure, they could sue Letherbee. But if other companies, like FEW, kept making products they called "Malört," where would it lead?

"I see no end to the trademark issue, unless you do, and I'm not sure what decision to make regarding this," she wrote to Bill O'Donaghue in late summer.

The only option, he said, was to keep fighting. Sure enough, the fight wore on—but only briefly. Letherbee signaled it planned to oppose Carl Jeppson Company's trademark application by asking the USPTO for an extension to formally do so.

However after extracting an extra six weeks to sell through its stock of R. Franklin's Original Label Malört, until mid-February 2014, it agreed to stop selling a product called "Malört" and not to further object to the trademark application. One problem was solved.

So was a second when FEW Spirits also agreed to stop selling anything called "Malört." FEW owner Paul Hletko called Bill O'Donaghue, ranted for ten minutes with a flurry of four-letter words, and suggested that Pat should sell him the brand. He issued an angry Tweet about the cease and desist ("Let your bartender know you don't appreciate Jeppson's threatening lawsuits over this stuff"). Then he signed a settlement. Hletko was confident he could win, but a lawsuit would be baggage he didn't need. He blacked out the word *Malört* on his remaining bottles of Anguish and Regret and sold them until they were gone.

The local rivals were vanquished. Yet a far larger problem loomed, an unforeseen competitor that would undoubtedly have the will and the means for a battle. It was one of the largest liquor companies in the world.

17

PAT AND SAM

PETER AND CHRIS spent months on it, pages of notes and ideas stuffed into a binder. It never took shape until October 2013, when both Bill O'Donaghue and Malört's Wirtz rep told Pat what Peter and Chris had said for months: it was time to move the company forward. They needed a plan.

Carl Jeppson Co. could no longer operate merely as George Brode's legacy. Too much was possible, too much at stake. Sales soared to new heights, and there was no reason to think it couldn't continue. The company required shape and direction to get there. It couldn't lurch from opportunity to opportunity, crisis to crisis. The company needed a plan. Wirtz wanted to see it in six weeks.

Knowing Peter and Chris were already at work on the bones of such a project, Pat agreed to pay Chris $500 to formalize the document. Her mounting legal bills meant she couldn't afford any more, she said.

Chris said $500 was fine. He didn't care much about the money. What he wanted was to lay out exactly what needed to happen if Carl Jeppson Co. was to grow with him and Peter involved. The dynamic had severed—Pat and Sam in one corner, Peter and Chris in the other—and plotting their vision was the only way forward.

Peter worried about being too blunt, about their plan creating an irreparable split. Chris insisted bluntness was the only way. Pat might go for the plan, and she might not. At least they would have their audience.

On an early Monday afternoon in December 2013, Peter and Chris sat down with Pat and Sam for an early dinner at a suburban Greek restaurant. Pat liked to do things early and to be home early, so they agreed to a 4:00 PM meeting.

After the waters were poured and the pleasantries exchanged, Peter and Chris slid copies of their proposal across the table. The cover, bearing Malört's unmistakable logo, read:

Jeppson's Malört
Moving Forward

Pat and Sam began picking through the eighteen pages, stunned at what they saw. Some of the recommendations were wholly uncontroversial, such as shifting the company email from Gmail to proper addresses with a Jeppsonsmalort.com domain. The rest of the document could barely hide Chris and Peter's dismay at the state of things.

A market analysis argued Malört attracted a "flippant" audience of younger drinkers drawn to its "exclusivity, shock value, edginess, and uniqueness." Letherbee, they noted, "takes themselves seriously" with a "professional looking" product. Chris had gently suggested for months that Pat consider updating Malört's bottle and label, retaining the historic charm while cleaning it up to modern design standards. Now he was pointed about it. The combination of its ordinary bottle, brown plastic cap and a busy label largely untouched since the 1950s could no longer compete: "It screams cheap," he said.

Malört's strengths amounted to four brief lines—seventeen words— that included the brand's "deep, cultural history" and "great, albeit small following." Its weaknesses stretched paragraphs across a full page. Malört, they said, was seen as "a novelty, fad, or a joke" with "too narrow of a focus."

"We have a loyal base, but it's too small to sustain Jeppson's Malört," they said. "We're fishing barrels instead of oceans."

And then there was Sam.

Also under the "Weaknesses" heading, Chris and Peter wrote: "We seem to have a reliance on comedic relief and because of that choice not many respect our product or truly understand it." They backhandedly lamented Pat's leadership, citing a "lack of internal process and pecking order" and "short-sighted decisions."

The conclusion? "Jeppson's cannot be the punchline of jokes any longer."

"The message starts with us and we're sending the wrong one," they wrote. "We need to educate and unify internally first, so we can educate and unify externally."

Going forward, they wanted to hitch the brand to its Chicago history, rather than have it function as a sign of hipster cool. And as Grey Goose vodka's identity was tied to its French roots and Fernet-Branca to Italy, they wanted to lean on Malört's Swedish origins—"from Sweden to the streets of Chicago," they explained. They suggested a mascot, maybe a Viking, or a man in lederhosen toasting a shot of Malört.

Rather than drilling into Malört as a dare or a joke, they said, opportunity lay simply in being the rare American-made besk: "That's a lot more unique and memorable than the self-deprecation that has become Jeppson's."

The last few pages offered additional surprises. Sam's shock came in the proposed leadership structure. Pat would be chief executive officer. Chris would be second in command as creative director and marketing manager. All ideas speaking to the world—ads, marketing, social media—would run through him.

It was a quietly radical suggestion; months earlier, Sam asked Pat if he could print business cards for himself. Sure, she said. He said he needed a title for the cards. Pat told him to give himself whatever title he wanted; titles meant nothing to her. Sam settled on creative director. Pat was fine with it. She thought he was the most creative member of the bunch anyway.

The problem, as Chris saw it, was that in most companies, creative director was a serious and lofty role, responsible for steering a brand through a world crowded with competitors. It required strategy and planning. It didn't amount to cheeky social media posts that occasionally had to be pulled down for offending customers. With ten years of marketing and design experience, Chris thought *he* was qualified for the role. Sam simply was not. And Pat was oblivious. The "master plan," as they called it, was Chris's moment to cement the responsibility he thought he'd earned.

Peter would be third in command as director of public relations, which meant handling all media interviews—something Sam had also increasingly done, including a high-profile television spot where he prodded the anchors to take their first shots of Malört live on air (to predictable lamentations). In Peter's hands, Malört as a live television stunt would be no more.

Left for Sam was fourth in the four-person company—director of social media and sales development. He'd work with the distributor to get Malört in bars and write Twitter and Facebook posts vetted by Chris.

As the food arrived, Sam couldn't eat. He lost his appetite.

Pat's shock came at the next page, under the heading "Budgets and Investments." The company needed "a realistic budget" and "serious marketing plan," Peter and Chris said. They wanted to move production to a local distillery to build credibility. There would be financial risk in upsetting the status quo, but they insisted it was time.

They also wanted jobs—maybe not immediately but eventually. Relying on volunteers was not sustainable, they said; it produced inconsistent work and left a negative image, "as though we don't believe in ourselves enough to invest in our company's future."

They proposed that Pat take on investors, partners, or a loan to allow for "full time employees or at the very least more consistent dedication to duties that need to be accomplished." Hiring full-time staff, they said, would also take "a tremendous amount of weight off of Pat's shoulders."

Pat kept a stony face throughout the two-hour meeting. She thanked Peter and Chris for their time.

That night she combed the document with a purple highlighter, underlining the words and phrases that seemed to say the most.

Shock value
Novelty, fad or a joke

Reliance on comedic relief
Not many respect our product or truly understand it
We're sending the wrong one
Self deprecation
Be edgy, but not lewd, crass or elitist

On page 15, she crossed out Sam's proposed title of social media director and scrawled beside his name his current role, the one Chris envisioned for himself: "Creative Director."

On the last page, she drew a slash through the proposal to take on investors or a loan. Beside it she wrote, "BS."

Pat emailed Sam days later, asking his thoughts on the master plan. She liked some of the ideas. Converting email to @jeppsonsmalort.com addresses made sense. She struggled with much of the rest of it.

"Are we a fad and a novelty?" she asked. "Should we push our Swedish origins? Does the label scream cheap?"

She told Sam she already made one decision. No loans, no partners. All she saw was risk.

"Putting more money into the company would not ensure an increase in sales and I would be responsible for payment of the loan," she wrote, "and if the investors lost money they would expect me to lose right along with them."

Sam replied unusually quickly, within hours, calling a response to the master plan "such a complex and gut-wrenching issue." There were indeed some good ideas, he said, but he rejected its tenor and approach.

It wasn't a plan, it was an ultimatum with our company's "salvation" as its hostage. The fact that they view us as a fad or a novelty and that they can "rescue us from that" is pretty insulting as well. George Brode knew, just as you and I do, that Malört is special because it is unique and because it is strong. It is a truly NOVEL thing, not a "novelty." . . .

I just think that it's time to take a closer look at the people who see themselves fit to serve you and to help you grow this brand, myself included. I just hope that everyone involved knows that vision, hard work, dedication, and honesty are all to be judged and that choices will be made.

Pat's reply: "I have avoided being confrontational with them up to now but I'm afraid the time has come."

On a Tuesday afternoon, nearly a month after sitting down with Peter and Chris, she sent her reply. Sam wrote most of it, which Pat lightly edited to her own voice. After weeks of stewing, the gut-wrenching decision turned to withering dismissal.

Pat said she was "overwhelmed by the cynical and negative way in which you view this product" and criticized the restructuring of power as sidelining her in her own company. She rejected the idea of taking on partners or a loan, accusing Peter and Chris of "naivete and blind entitlement."

The email concluded: "You are volunteers, yet I feel as though you have lost sight of your roles. You can either return to that original arrangement, or you can apply your efforts to something else you find more worthy of your time."

She clicked send. A minute later she forwarded the email to Sam.

"The die is cast," she said. "I hope you have someone who can teach you how to run a website."

Simpler days seemed to be ahead. Peter and Chris were likely to move on. The small, local distillers gave up the fight for the word *Malört*.

Then, a week after the showdown over gyros and saganaki, came a letter from Sazerac, a $4.5 billion spirits company, addressed to Bill McGrath. The Louisiana-based owner of more than four hundred liquor brands invoked an argument even Pat and Bill O'Donaghue once believed: *Malört* was a descriptive term. It therefore could not be trademarked.

> Although Sazerac has no objection to your client using
> the word "Malört" in identifying the type of liquor your
> client markets and sells, the word is generic for a specific
> type of distilled spirit and is not registerable as a trademark
> for liquor.
>
> Sazerac markets various spirits, including vodka, whis-
> key, tequila and various liqueurs. If Carl Jeppson is allowed
> to register "Malört" for liquor, Sazerac and other compet-
> itors within the alcoholic beverages industry will be pre-
> vented from using the word "Malört" to accurately describe
> products or beverages containing Malört.

Sazerac pointed to R. Franklin's as proof, calling it "a type of Malört."

"Accordingly," the letter concluded, "Sazerac respectfully requests that
Carl Jeppson expressly abandon its application for Malört." It asked for
"written assurance" within three weeks that the trademark application
would be withdrawn.

Bill McGrath was stunned. Sazerac? Caring about a tiny local operation making a single, strange, hard-to-drink brand with modest sales?
Why would Sazerac battle over something so few people enjoyed?

Yet it seemed primed for battle, and to Pat it felt dire. It wasn't the
thujone scare of seven years earlier. That felt like the end of it all. But
if *Malört* was found to be generic, there would be half a dozen imitators
within a year. Her brand's value would plummet—and the value of the
company *was* the value of the brand.

Bill McGrath declined Sazerac's request. He used Peter Strom's old
argument: Malört was a form of besk, which made R. Franklin's an
attempt "to try to ride on the coattails of Jeppson's goodwill." In fact,
he said, Letherbee would be dropping its use of the word; Robby and
Brenton had signed a settlement agreement the week before. It would be
changing the name to R. Franklin's Original Recipe Besk.

"To the best of our knowledge, Sazerac has successfully operated for
many years without referring to bask brannvin products as 'malort,' so we
fail to perceive any harm to Sazerac or any other companies if Jeppson's
Malört mark is registered," Bill wrote.

For more than two months, that was the end of it. Then, in February 2014, the last day of its window to oppose the trademark, Sazerac did it. Just as Pat calculated that Letherbee couldn't stand the fight against a larger company with a pricey liquor lawyer, Sazerac seemed to presume the same of Pat. It was one of the world's largest liquor companies. She was a one-woman operation, running a company from her apartment. How could *she* battle *them*?

They weren't wrong.

It was left to Bill McGrath to let Pat know that Sazerac planned to follow through.

"Sorry to report the bad news," he told her.

———————

Chris took a night to compose himself after Pat's rebuke. He didn't plan to write so much in response, but the thoughts kept churning, a year of reckoning come due. He defended his intentions as "honest and good," and bristled at the idea that he and Peter were out for their own gain, as Sam suggested while hashing out the reply.

In fact, Chris said, he had the least on the line of anyone. He already had a stable job. The master plan, he said, was a "completely fair and well thought out document that wasn't concerned with people's feelings." The goal, he said, was simply to grow the company.

Chris continued:

> We have always had yours and Jeppson's better interest
> in mind with EVERYTHING we've done. I am very sad
> that you cannot see how true our intentions were all along.
>
> But alas, such is life. Not everyone sees things from the
> same perspective. And to me that has been the biggest road-
> block. You, Sam, and Peter and I all have different visions.
> We all want Jeppson's to grow, but we all have drastically
> different ideas and approaches to that end goal. That is
> why I am going to very humbly step back and allow you

and Sam to proceed with a path that is more comfortable
for you guys and your vision.

He said he hoped they'd stay in touch. Pat responded during one of
her sleepless nights, just before 4:00 AM, to say she also wanted to "stay
friends and stay in touch"—though they didn't.

Peter's reply came two days later. It was far more abrupt. "I guess
I'm done," he said. "I apologize for being a bad volunteer. I'm sorry for
all the hours, days, work days, and money I put into this effort to make
you and Malört more successful."

Pat responded quickly to say she hoped Peter would stay on as Malört's
resident historian, "which is, of course, your forte." She signed the email
"Love, Pat."

Peter didn't reply for more than two weeks, until after Christmas
and New Year's.

"I've thought about continuing on as historian a lot lately," he finally
wrote on a frigid Tuesday morning. "This project is my passion and
you are my friend, but I think it's best if I take a step back at this time.

"I would like to be away from Malört for a while."

For thirty-three years George and Pat ran Jeppson's Malört. Now it was
Pat and Sam. It was a relief.

The demands of success weren't going away. Neither was Sazerac.
The resentments were at least resolved. The quiet jockeying for position
among Pat's boys had grown exhausting. Now she was down to one boy,
one she admired and trusted.

And Sam was finally free to craft Malört's vision. Peter and Chris
always seemed ready for him to fail or else to squash his ideas. Now it
was his story to tell. That would mean less talk of Carl Jeppson and
Malört's Swedish heritage, more talk of the oddball thing it had become
in Chicago bars. It wasn't that Sam didn't care about the legacy; he just
thought it could wait. Its more recent history was what resonated among
the new generation of fans. What mattered, he thought, was how Malört

made those people *feel*—the interactions it created and the conversations it started.

The ideas came furiously. Less than a month after Peter and Chris departed, Sam announced a contest on Malört's social media channels: in 250 words or less, explain "why are you the best person on earth to receive a free Malört tattoo." Malört's authenticity and outsider status made it not only a darling of the bars but also the rare brand people committed to their skin. Sam had seen or heard of more than a dozen Malört tattoos across the city, and it was exactly the sort of trend he wanted to turn into marketing, a stunt he promised Pat could go viral.

Nearly 150 entries poured in. Some were just a few sentences, or silly poems that could easily be cast aside. Others told stories humorous (a blind date abruptly ended when the other party claimed to hate Malört) or heartfelt (pouring the liqueur on the grave of a dead relative).

Sam read the essays. He read them again. He and Pat sat down at her dining room table on a snowy January evening and dug through the pile. She thought the contest was a silly idea initially, but flipping through the essays, she was touched and surprised by how meaningful Malört could be to people.

They finally settled on one from Wyl Villacres, a recent fiction-writing graduate who discovered Malört as a twenty-one-year-old without much money, drawn in by a neighborhood bar that sold two-dollar "flu shots" that turned out to be Malört. Wyl latched on immediately. He was a heavy smoker who found that the strange, bitter liquor reached his palate like few other things. He could down shots with barely a grimace, becoming "the Malört fan" among his friends. When the contest was announced, a dozen friends sent him the link. It was all of his favorite things: Malört, tattoos, and writing. Wyl wrote three drafts of his essay, trying to emulate the voice Sam had built for the brand on social media, which Wyl later described for a reporter as "this sort of dry, crass sense of humor." He wrote:

> I live a mile away from the hospital I was born in. I suf-
> fer with the other Cubs fans every fucking year. I give
> directions in colors and/or numbers. I know how to not

get frostbite when the temperature is below zero and beer runs still need to be made. I can get drunk anywhere in this city and still make it home easily. And I drink Malört like prohibition is starting again.

Malört is as Chicago as it gets (even if it is made in Florida). We're a city that doesn't pussyfoot around. We're tough, gritty, and take no shit. We're a boxer throwing body punches. We'd rather work and fight than try to get lucky with a prayer of a haymaker. We're shockingly bitter but bright and light underneath. Just like Malört. That's why I want to wear Malört on me forever. To remember who I am and where I'm from.

So delete the other emails. Let's inject ink into my skin and drink till it's numb.

A few months later Villacres redeemed his prize on the back of his left arm, just above the elbow, pounding a shot of Malört before, during, and after the needle. The tattoo artist got so much media coverage out of it that he didn't charge Sam for the work.

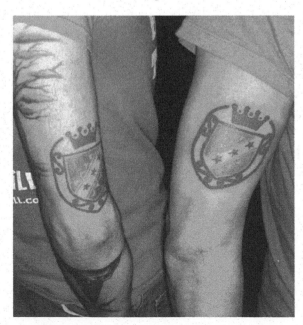

Malört tattoo contest winner Wyl Villacres (left) ran into someone inspired to get the same tattoo as him after seeing coverage of it in local media. *Courtesy of Wyl Villacres*

Sam followed the tattoo contest with another idea he nursed for more than a year: a Malört song. Its roots stretched to when he illicitly operated the Malört Facebook account, before the company launched a website or email address. There was nowhere else for questions and proposals, so they landed in Sam's direct messages.

Among the most intriguing was from local rock band Archie Powell & the Exports. One drunken night, a band member sent a message asking when they would be commissioned to write an official Malört song. Sam checked out the band and liked what he heard—brisk, sprightly pop-punk songs that certainly embodied Malört's spirit—but he didn't bother responding. There was nothing to say.

Finally, by fall 2013, with the title of creative director on his business card, he reached out to Archie to rekindle the idea. In addition to a few hundred dollars for studio time and mixing, Sam said, Carl Jeppson Co. could offer T-shirts for the band and a case of Malört to take on tour. Archie and the band eagerly accepted.

Sam emailed Pat, Peter, and Chris to say the band was working on an ode to Malört. Peter and Chris didn't even bother responding; they were deep into their master plan, unconcerned with what they considered Sam's latest distraction.

With Peter and Chris gone, though, Sam could go all in on the project, even filming and editing a music video. He played an early version of the song for Pat, just Archie singing while strumming an acoustic guitar. Pat thought it sounded like bad folk music.

When she heard the amped-up full-band version months later, she was dazzled. "The Malört Song (A Waltz for Old Jeppson)" was raucous and joyful, launching with a touch of feedback before soaring through three anthemic minutes of Malört-fueled joy: "I'll buy a Jeppson's for everyone here at the bar / And a Jeppson's for you and for me / Because whether you like it or think it bizarre / Has got nothing to do with the deed" went the chorus.

Sam spent two months hauling cameras around the city to shoot the video: the band of lightly scruffy guys in T-shirts and hoodies in its practice space; loving shots of Chicago's skyline and barrooms; three different Malört tattoos (including Wyl Villacres's and Brad Bolt's); and of course Pat, dressed in a black turtleneck and purple corduroy jacket, autographing a bottle of Malört at Paddy Long's.

The song garnered a bit of media coverage ("'The Malort Song' is Archie Powell's most bitter release," said the *Chicago Tribune*) and lived on the internet, but it fell short of Sam's dreams of defining both the band and the brand. Still, like the tattoo contest, it was a turning point—a declaration of Sam's vision, a show of what he could do with a chance. Malört gave him purpose. His family saw him swell with pride. His focus became the most acute they'd seen. With the weight of the company shifted to his shoulders, edgy quips and photoshopped billboards wouldn't suffice. He knew he had to do better.

————————

In a sense, by 2014 it barely mattered who was at the controls. It could have been Peter and Chris or Pat and Sam or whoever, really. The world had woken up to Jeppson's Malört. Largely confined to the outliers fifteen years earlier, any self-respecting Chicago bar—especially those appealing to young professionals, the artistically inclined, and recent college graduates—simply had to have a bottle at the ready.

After a record-setting 2013 (4,584 cases sold), accounts new and old pushed Jeppson's Malört to even grander heights in 2014 (5,617 cases sold). Bars that wouldn't have bothered with Malört just a few years earlier were good for at least a bottle or two a week.

The owner of Christina's Place, where Peter Strom had convinced the owner to carry Malört a couple of years earlier, told the *Chicago Tribune* he barely sold Malört in 2012. By 2013 it had grown so popular, he began stacking the empty bottles along a wall near the front door.

"It started as a joke," he told the newspaper. "Now we don't put 'em up anymore because we sell so many."

By the end of the year, Christina's tore through four or five bottles of Malört every weekend—on par with Jose Cuervo, Jim Beam, and Jack Daniel's. One customer ordered it mixed with ginger ale.

"I had to taste it for myself," the bar's owner told the *Tribune*. "It's actually nice and drinkable."

Bottles of Jeppson's Malört lined up for weekend service at Bar DeVille.
Courtesy of Brad Bolt

Sam, who updated his title to director of marketing, sent letters to such newer customers with the typical wink, saying Carl Jeppson Co. "would like to commend you on your decision to purchase Malört, the most infamous liquor on earth. Bold move . . . bold move indeed." By the middle of 2014, he sent a stack of the letters weekly.

The biggest surge happened in the longtime accounts. Bar DeVille went from pouring two bottles of Malört a week in 2009 to nine bottles a week in 2014. The Green Mill no longer had to foist Malört on unsuspecting guests; now the guests asked for it, which returned the old jazz club to its throne as the city's top Malört account, plowing through more than a case a week. At the end of the year, Pat sent a letter of gratitude, which Green Mill owner Dave Jemilo promptly framed and hung behind the bar.

> To the Men and Women of The Green Mill:
> We are deeply honored to announce that for the year 2014
> The Green Mill sold more Jeppson's Malört than any other

bar or liquor store in the world. Beyond this annual accolade, it also bears mention that for the last century your extraordinary staff has sold more Malört than any other single entity on the planet. For that there is no "thank you" worthy of your service.

Distribution continued to expand (to Maryland), and media continued to catch on. *Eater* gave Malört to ten New York City sommeliers ("They must be even more miserable in Chicago than I thought," one said). The *Onion* gave it to unsuspecting musical acts at Riot Fest. (Chicago bands knew it well; bands from out of town were generally confused or revolted.)

Malört came to loom large in the public consciousness, enough to seem larger than it was. Riot Fest offered the chance to be a VIP sponsor for $25,000. Sam just laughed. Malört had nowhere close to that kind of marketing budget. In reality Pat remained the only full-time employee, though Sam did finally graduate from volunteer to part-time.

———————————

Sazerac had Cooley LLP in its corner, an international firm with offices around the globe and a client list packed with billion-dollar companies.

Pat had Bill McGrath and his firm of five lawyers.

The sides finally talked over the phone in April 2014, five months after Sazerac signaled it would oppose the trademark. Expect interviews and depositions for Pat and others from the company, they said. There would also be copious documents requests and third-party depositions (Bill guessed they might try to use Letherbee to their advantage). Sazerac didn't explain its interest in the term *Malört* but was clear it had no interest in settling.

Other than an article in the *Chicago Tribune*, the skirmish generally escaped public notice. Behind the scenes, Pat was a wreck. Sales continued to grow, but her stack of legal bills kept pace. Battling Sazerac, as Sazerac likely knew, hobbled her in a way that it didn't a conglomerate. Bill warned her that that was probably the plan: large companies were often content simply to outlast smaller ones. Sometimes it wasn't about who was right. It was about who had the appetite for the fight.

The fight cost Pat $2,000 to $5,000 dollars a month—a stunning fee to her and barely a rounding error to Sazerac. When a particularly weighty bill arrived, Bill added a note explaining he wrote some time off, but they were in a time-intensive stage of the case, combing through years of documents and correspondence. He promised future months wouldn't be so bad.

"I hope this is not wreaking too much havoc on Jeppson," he said. He followed with a stack of documents for Pat to review, twenty-five pages thick, which he said "probably read like a lot of legal mumbo jumbo"—and indeed it did as she combed through it on a Friday evening in her condo over a glass of wine.

Back and forth the sides went across months. Sazerac argued *malort* (always lowercase) was "a generic term for a kind of drink." Look no further, they said, than the words entering pop culture in recent years: *Malörtiness*, *Malört-ology*, and naturally, *Malörtface*. Bill insisted generic uses of *Malört* (always uppercase) referred specifically to Jeppson's.

Sazerac argued the emergence of "malört" spirits from Letherbee and FEW further proved the term was generic. Bill swatted that argument away easily; those companies had already agreed to cease and desist. He hired Anne-Marie Andreasson-Hogg, the North Park University Swedish professor Peter Strom recommended a couple of years earlier, to explore the meaning of the word *malört* in Swedish and extrapolate its uniqueness to Carl Jeppson Co. in English.

After consulting six Swedish dictionaries, she concluded at the end of a forty-page report, "Without any doubt . . . *malört* does not have the meaning of 'alcoholic drink' by itself. A second word denoting drink must be present for such a meaning." Bill entered the report as evidence.

In fall Bill got an unexpected call from one of Sazerac's lawyers. They chatted for half an hour. She seemed to be fishing around about the possibility of settling. It was interesting, he thought; six months earlier they seemed to have no willingness to settle. He wondered if Pat's months of resolve had changed Sazerac's calculation.

Sazerac's lawyer followed up a month later with a two-page letter. In the last paragraph, she again made the suggestion: "We remain open to discussing an amicable resolution of this matter. If your client would like to engage in settlement negotiations, please let me know." Otherwise, she said, Sazerac would proceed with a trial. She asked for dates Pat would be available for a deposition.

If they were trying to scare a poor old lady, it worked. Talking to a room of distributors scared Pat. This would be infinitely more terrifying. What if she said the wrong thing? What if that wrong thing doomed her company? She was already a fitful sleeper; the thought of testifying, of her words entering a court transcript, had her pacing the condo night after night and typing 3:00 AM emails to her attorneys. Interest in a settlement offered hope, but it wasn't as if she could give up protecting the word *Malört*.

"I suppose it's like believing in Santa Claus or the Easter Bunny to think that at this point Sazerac would back off," she emailed Bill.

Sazerac didn't back off. Its attorneys spent another six months collecting evidence and threatening to depose Pat. The firm was particularly interested in correspondence going back years within Carl Jeppson Co. and how it used the word *Malört*—generically or only as a proper name?

As part of its discovery, Sazerac wanted documents from not only Pat and Sam but also Peter Strom. Almost a year and a half had passed since he left the company, and it continued to be a painful separation. He avoided Malört's growing avalanche of media coverage. So much of it focused on Sam.

Now Sazerac wanted to know what he knew. While working at the church one afternoon, Peter was served a request for twenty-one different types of documents, most of them pertaining to how Peter had used the word word *Malört* in company communications. He was equally surprised and angry that Pat or Sam hadn't warned him, and also scared, wondering what to do. He called a lawyer who wrote wills for his family. The lawyer's first question was simple: How deeply did Peter want to get involved?

He instinctively, desperately wanted to be involved. It was the very subject he spent months fighting for and was repeatedly told no. More than wanting to be involved, though, he *didn't* want to be involved. He was still bitter. He was still done.

The lawyer advised him to keep things tidy and send every email he had—from his first meeting with Pat, when she expected to encounter

an old man, to the squabbles about Sam to Peter's seething insistence of
the thing Pat was now trying to prove. He knew his arguments for the
trademark were all over those emails and might help Pat's case. At least
his arguments would finally be heard.

He printed the emails, hundreds and hundreds of them, stuffed them
into an envelope, and sent them off.

On a Wednesday in late June, Pat took the bus down Lake Shore Drive
to Bill O'Donaghue's office. Sazerac's Chicago-based global sales director
wanted to meet. He was also an executive member of the mergers and
acquisitions team.

Bill had little idea what to expect but was open to a discussion if it
could lead to resolution. The meeting stretched more than an hour, and
the Sazerac representative eventually got to the point. As Bill would recall,
he was told they'd drop the legal battle if Pat sold the company to them.

It was a lightbulb moment for Bill. Suddenly it all made sense. A big
guy saw a little guy having success. The big guy wanted it for himself.

Bill said the meeting was done. They'd be happy to litigate.

For weeks, silence followed.

Sazerac had an early September deadline to share the evidence and
witnesses it would offer at trial. It missed the deadline.

Neither Bill O'Donaghue nor Bill McGrath were sure what to make
of that. Ten days later they found out. Without a word of explanation,
Sazerac's attorneys withdrew their opposition to the trademark. It was
suddenly, miraculously over.

Malört was Jeppson's alone.

They celebrated with a fancy Italian meal downtown: both Bills, their
wives, Sam, and Pat. There was no Malört on hand but plenty of wine.
Even after tens of thousands of dollars in legal bills, Pat was so relieved
that she insisted on picking up the check.

18

AND NOW IT'S GONE

Malört remained a punch line. Finally, it was in on the joke.

Thanks to George's decades of steadfast stewardship and Pat's years of steering the ship when there barely seemed a reason; thanks to Peter and Chris dragging Malört into the twenty-first century and Sam's creativity and daring; thanks to changing tastes and the cocktail revolution, Malört would not only never be an afterthought again, it had become a muse.

A theology doctoral candidate launched a Malört 5K race in 2014 as a fundraiser for a Chicago food depository. Participants got a shot before the starting whistle and another at the finish line (plus a can of beer). The first-place finisher won a bottle of Jeppson's Malört. The last-place finisher got two.

Robbie Ellis, a humorous songwriter and classical music DJ, wrote a jaunty tune about Malört shortly after moving to Chicago from New Zealand in 2015, discovering it on a first date. The six verses in "A Shot of Malört" were sung from the perspectives of different characters new to Chicago, each of whom found their place in the city by slugging down a shot of Malört ("A shot of Malört will make you feel new / A shot of Malört puts Chicago into you"). Ellis didn't particularly care for Malört, but he thought it a perfect lens to reflect his new hometown.

That same year in Los Angeles, Malört became a staple of *Heidi & Frank Mornings*, on rock station 95.5 KLOS, after a producer from

Chicago insisted he knew the world's worst-tasting liquor. No one believed him, so they ordered a bottle. Sure enough, they couldn't believe what they tasted. The result was an on-air quiz show called "The Malört Challenge" in which wrong answers were punished with shots of Malört. The audience couldn't get enough of it.

Hunter Hobbs, a budding social media influencer in Norman, Oklahoma, tracked down a bottle after hearing about it on *Heidi & Frank Mornings*. He also thought Malört was terrible but became inspired to make a YouTube video of college friends from different countries trying it for the first time.

"It tastes like lead pencil!" sputtered an Australian woman.

"I want to cut my tongue off a little bit," said a man from the Netherlands.

"Who are you, Carl Jeppson?" an exasperated British man asked. "The question I have is, when he made it, how did he go, 'Yeah, that's good?'"

Hobbs racked up nearly five hundred thousand views.

Malört had grown iconic—even in places it couldn't be bought.

A more ambitious company would have seized on the momentum with at least four or five people navigating the growing to-dos. Instead, the inner circle remained tight: Pat at the controls, her salary finally creeping up to put her mind at ease, and Sam handling most of the details. Short of writing checks or placing orders with Florida Distillers, Pat was happy to let Sam take on as much responsibility as he pleased. She introduced him to people as her "right-hand young man."

Sam relished the opportunity. He was the gatekeeper, the boots on the ground, the first to learn a particular Walgreens started tagging Malört bottles with anti-theft collars because they were disappearing so regularly—the highest of compliments, he told Pat.

Sam planned events, stayed in touch with distributors, fielded media inquiries, and guided the marketing strategy. The more responsibility he had, the more he thought as Peter and Chris did before leaving the company, that Malört couldn't only be a prank or a dare. If it was never taken seriously, most people would try it once and then never again. As marketing director, he realized, his job was to drive Malört deeper into the city's psyche as something meaningful and lasting. In 2015, that led to his most enduring effort, the introduction of the "Chicago Handshake"—a can of the city's most iconic budget beer, Old Style, alongside a shot of Malört. It was a simple idea that gave bargoers a new context to appreciate Malört. It was a quick hit across the city.

Sam didn't commemorate his love for Malört with a tattoo. Anyone could get a Malört tattoo. He did one better: he cruised around town in George's massive old Lincoln Continental—which Pat gave him—with a one-of-a-kind "MALORT" license plate that generated honks from passing cars and thumbs-ups from bikers. Friends and acquaintances texted him photos of his own license plate, not realizing it was his.

Sam also plunged deeper into sales, including a weekly Tuesday drive to Wisconsin to shoehorn Malört into ever more accounts. He'd regularly get five, seven, or even ten new bars in a week. He always followed up with a T-shirt of gratitude in the mail.

Merchandise became almost as lucrative as Malört itself: five-dollar shot glasses, fifteen-dollar knit caps, T-shirts ranging from sixteen to twenty-two dollars, and hoodies that cost a whopping forty-two dollars. As the appetite for Malört merch grew fierce, the company branched out, including a thirty-dollar candle made from a reclaimed Malört bottle and a forty-two-dollar flag. One-third of sales happened between Thanksgiving and Christmas, often more than a hundred orders a day, slowing only as they ran out of the most popular sizes.

Pat initially handled the orders, but only until the piles grew across her office floor and the task overwhelmed her. After she tripped over a stack of sweatshirts and wrenched her back, Sam took over that work too. He built shelves in his apartment to keep the orders organized.

In 2015 *Thrillist* named Sam's job one of the best in the city ("11 Cool Chicago Jobs You'd Take in a Heartbeat"), joining the Chicago Cubs' scoreboard operator and a guy who owned some of the coolest rock clubs in town. Beneath a photo of Sam gently kissing a bottle of Malört as if it were a newborn, he compared his unusual route to working for the company to "seeing Radiohead in concert and they ask you to come up and play keyboards." The tattoo contest and music video were examples of what he called "complete creative freedom to shape the direction of one of Chicago's most iconic brands."

"I'm deeply honored to be a part of a company that bold and that crazy," he said.

It wasn't the company that was that bold and that crazy. It was Sam. There may not have been a more conservative business owner in the world of alcohol than Pat. But she trusted Sam and admired his creative mind. She knew he understood how Malört thrived in a way she couldn't. So she let him do what he wanted.

Sam slowly became one with Malört's narrative, hailed as a hero for ushering it to modern-day relevance. The swelling coverage typically skated over Carl Jeppson and George Brode. Pat usually merited no more than a passing reference. Peter and Chris were written out of the story entirely. Sam's origin with Malört—from rogue social media accounts to face of the company—was an irresistible backstory for such an unlikely renaissance.

One podcaster prefaced an interview with Sam in 2016 by describing him as "the heart and soul of the brand," crediting him as "largely responsible for its resurgence as a beloved Chicago institution."

Sam gladly played the role. It was literally his dream come true. He couldn't help continuing to dream.

"Maybe someday I'll be overseeing the production of it here in Chicago," he said on the podcast. "It's gonna happen. It's just a question of when."

And why not? As Pat entered her seventies without a succession plan, she did what seemed obvious. Just as George left Carl Jeppson Co. to her in his will, she left it to Sam.

Forget keyboards. It was like going to a Radiohead show and being invited onstage to sing, play guitar, *and* write the songs.

––––––––––

The rare issue to unite Peter, Chris, and Sam for the year and a half they worked together was a belief that Jeppson's Malört needed to come home.

Central Florida production was fine when no one paid attention and sales sputtered. Now that sales surged and everyone seemed to be paying attention, Malört's twelve-hundred-mile journey to the bars of Chicago worked against it—especially in the era of "craft" and "local." Sam got

Malört into new accounts every week, but holdouts remained. The most ideological bar owners said they loved Malört and its place in Chicago culture, but they couldn't sell it because it wasn't *really* local.

The only solution was to move production closer to home. As early as 2012, they began looking for a new distiller. There weren't many in Chicago, so they looked across the state. There weren't many in Illinois either, so they looked beyond state lines. Key for Pat was finding a partner that could guide Malört through its entire process—secure the neutral spirit base, handle the wormwood, bottle the finished product, label the bottles, box them up, and ship to the suburban warehouse Pat rented. She demanded a seamless transition from Florida Distillers.

In summer 2013, after a presentation to the company's Wisconsin distributors, Pat's Wirtz rep arranged a visit to another of its brands, Death's Door, a distillery just outside Madison. Pat was exhausted from the three-hour ride and the nerves that accompanied talking to a room full of strangers. She was in no mood for a distillery tour, especially because no one told her the reason for it. Halfway through, it struck her—this could be a new home for Jeppson's Malört.

She exchanged emails for months with the owner of Death's Door, a process of smiles and optimism early on. When Pat detected hedging on a commitment to bottling and labeling, she demanded assurance. Death's Door backed out of the talks.

Pat was disappointed, fretting she overplayed her hand. In another sense, it was just as well. Florida Distillers was what she knew, and what she knew worked. She worried that a smaller, newer distillery such as Death's Door would go out of business and leave her stranded. (In 2018 Pat's concern was validated; Death's Door did go out of business.)

They later looked at a distillery in Iowa near the Illinois border. Those talks also didn't get far. Finally, in late 2014, Sam got a text message from Tremaine Atkinson, who had opened CH Distillery in downtown Chicago the previous year.

CH Distillery was a cozy spot, a short walk to high-rise apartments and thousands of offices that filled every weekday with commuters. Most young distilleries focused on gin and whiskey—bolder flavors that dovetailed with the craft movement. Tremaine fixed largely on vodka. It was his preferred spirit and, he thought, a way to differentiate from the wave of young distilleries. What bar or restaurant didn't churn through an ocean of vodka?

Tremaine, knowing he couldn't build a distillery on vodka alone, was always looking for his next move. He saw it while chatting with a luminary from Chicago's wine industry, who said Malört was trying to bring production back home. He gave Tremaine Sam's number. Said maybe there could be a fit.

Tremaine sent Sam a text message in the following days, inviting him to CH. Sam came by, tasting CH spirits and touring the space. Pat eventually came by too. She appreciated Tremaine's interest, but saw no way this tiny distillery could possibly handle the needs of Carl Jeppson Company.

Tremaine started visiting Paddy Long's one Sunday afternoon a month to maintain the relationship and to keep the possibility of making Malört alive. He found Sam charming, knowledgeable, and gracious—a quintessential Chicago bartender. Sam enjoyed the visits too. Tremaine seemed grounded—warm, sincere, and eager to learn about the industry he joined. He wanted to take over production, but his interest didn't seem opportunistic; it was clearly rooted in admiration for Malört's odd coolness factor and intrinsic Chicago connection. Sam poured him new batches and past vintages, explaining the nuances. Tremaine kept at it, visiting Sam monthly and updating his proposals for Pat a couple times a year. She never said yes. But she also never quite said no.

———————

The old-timers—Karl at the bar, nursing stomach problems and watching *Jeopardy!*—always drank Jeppson's Malört.

The new generation of early adopters—art students like Katherine Raz and her pals—stumbled onto it in the old-man bars during the 1990s and early 2000s.

The bartenders—Brad Bolt and his cocktail renaissance ilk—found Malört around 2007.

The rest of the world woke up to it in 2012, pushing sales to heights not seen in forty years. It wasn't just the drinkers or the bartenders who caught on. It was the dealers and the dreamers too.

First was Larry Gutkin, a serial entrepreneur who talked a good game. He called Pat early that June, a moment when Pat felt good and open to the possibilities. Peter and Chris were helping, and Sam just joined the team. The first Malört event, at Nisei Lounge, was the previous week. The *Wall Street Journal* article seemed imminent.

Larry explained that he spent weeks in Manhattan and weekends in the Chicago suburbs. He'd been involved in many businesses, he said, including the company that made the famed Lava Lamps, after a private equity firm bought the floundering business in 2008 and installed him as CEO.

Pat was impressed enough by his résumé to invite him to come by the apartment on a Saturday morning. They talked for two hours. Larry told Pat he tried Jeppson's Malört at a Chicago rock club and marveled at how radically different it was. It deserved a wider audience, he said. He wanted to start in New York City.

Larry was confident and charming, though Pat was a bit skeptical of his tales of business acumen and the money he'd made—"kind of like a gambler that never tells you about his losses," she later told her lawyer.

After New York, Gutkin said, he wanted to take Jeppson's Malört national, maybe even international. He said he could put together a group of investors to make it happen, and that growth would cost them some of the early adopters, but they'd more than make up for the lost business with a vast new audience.

He reinvigorated Lava Lamps not because he was an expert in novelty lighting but because he understood what he called "the DNA of the brand." He believed he had a similar understanding of Jeppson's Malört.

"I do believe its time has come," he wrote in a follow-up email thanking Pat for her time. "As I told you before I left on Saturday, I have no doubt that you are on the verge of a big growth period. I do look forward to seeing that growth, and hope that you will allow me the privilege of being part of it."

They arranged a meeting at Bill's office and drew up a nondisclosure agreement to discuss terms. Pat seemed hopeful something might come from it, but the time between Larry's emails grew longer. Finally, he stopped responding and moved on to other ideas. Pat was briefly disappointed but soon forgot about him.

A few months later, in early 2013, came Dan Nagel, who sent a letter to Pat's condo. He learned of Malört in summer 1994, he said, after a Cubs game with his friend, the friend's father, and the friend's uncle, Dana. In the Wrigleyville bars after the game, Dan had his first Malört shot.

"I thought it tasted awful, but it has become an enduring memory for me," he wrote. Uncle Dana died in a car accident a few weeks later, he said, and Dan and his friend toasted the occasional shot of Malört in his memory.

Then he got to the point. "When I looked into the Carl Jeppson Company I learned of the work you have done since the passing of George Brode to keep Malört available to its followers," he wrote. "I would like to ask to meet with you at your convenience to discuss the possibility of purchasing the Carl Jeppson Company. I believe I would be an excellent steward of the tradition he passed on to you."

Dan attached his résumé, two dense pages that showed his current job as marketing manager at an industrial machinery manufacturer.

Pat sent Dan a polite letter thanking him for his interest but saying she was not interested in selling the company.

"Thank you for sharing the story with me about your introduction to Jeppson's Malört," she said. "Your Malört toasts are a great way to remember Uncle Dana."

A couple months later came Sam Hergott. He left phone messages. He sent letters. He said he was a devoted Malört fan who wanted "the opportunity to sit down and discuss the product and business with you." Pat ignored him. Sam kept after her with humor and his attempt at charm. In a follow-up letter, he said he was not "too proud to bribe or brown nose, so I've included five dollars, and might I add that you look lovely today."

Pat still ignored him. So he faxed a photo of a forlorn kitten.

> Pat,
> I've left voicemails, I've sent letters, I've even tried bribing
> you with a crisp five dollar bill (ok, it wasn't that crisp),
> yet I can't seem to get you to call or email me.

I'm running out of options, so I'm going to have to pull out the ace from my sleeve: <u>I'm faxing you a sad kitten.</u>

Look at that kitten's face. It is so sad. All that kitten wants is for you to reach out to me. Such a simple gesture will change this kitten's life. One call or email is all it will take.

I hope to hear from you soon. I want to see that kitten smile again.

Finally, Pat responded. As was her way, she sent a letter. As was also her way, she got to the point.

Dear Sam:
While I admire your tenacity, unfortunately I do not have any time to meet with you.

I suggest you put any business proposal you may have in detail and mail it to me.
Very truly yours,
Patricia D. Gabelick

So he did. With a more formal tone, he said he and his business partner were "loyal fans of the product for many years" but knew little of the backstory before the *Wall Street Journal* article. The article gave them the idea to buy the company.

Sam figured, rightly, that the swelling attention had already led to Pat being approached about selling. Also rightly, he said he and his partner "have a feeling that you would not sell this company to just any buyer—you want to ensure that, in the event of a sale, the legacy of the Carl Jeppson Company is protected."

He offered to earn her trust with a deal that would give them distribution rights in Wisconsin and Minnesota for one year. Perhaps then she would know their intentions were sincere.

"We know that Jeppson's appeals to a certain person, and that it isn't a product that one 'markets,'" he said. "It is a grass-roots campaign."

Ten days later Pat replied, again by letter, saying her brand was already poised to enter Wisconsin. "If you had just told me what you wanted in the beginning you would have saved both of us a lot of time," she wrote. "As you have already probably guessed, I do not want to sell the company at this time."

One person who didn't ask to buy the company was Tremaine Atkinson. He was playing the long game.

———————

Tremaine came from a family of achievers.

One brother was a trial attorney who excelled in several sports and recorded four CDs of original music. Another brother worked on Wall Street. His mother was an English teacher who went to law school in her forties and earned a clerkship with a federal judge in Oregon. His father was a Harvard University graduate who earned a PhD in physics from Stanford University, then taught at Washington University in St. Louis—where Tremaine was born in 1964—and Tufts University. In the 1970s he pivoted to a career in marketing, where he was early to applying computers and data to the field. He was also a skilled jazz pianist, often jamming late into the evening in the house as his kids drifted off to sleep.

Tremaine, too, was an achiever. He was a good student and bored easily. His parents split when he was a high school sophomore and sent him to Phillips Academy in Andover, Massachusetts, one of the nation's elite boarding schools. He grew his hair long like his rock 'n' roll hero, Jimmy Page, and learned to play guitar. He was kicked out of school after two years for smashing his instrument on stage during a battle of the bands, a final straw for a student whose middling attitude led to a calculus teacher accusing him of behaving like a "blasé oaf" from the back of the class, even as Tremaine got an A in the subject. For his last year of high school, he moved to Portland to live with his mother.

Tremaine spent three years at Pitzer College outside Los Angeles, where he was the best classical guitarist on campus. He thought he might make a career of it and transferred to the University of California San Diego, which had an elite program. He went last among a dozen people auditioning and, by the fourth performer, knew he wouldn't get in—and he didn't. He became an economics major.

After graduation and a year working in London, he took a job in San Francisco with Wells Fargo, as an investment accountant calculating fund values. He liked the work and he was good at it, seeing puzzles in the numbers waiting to be solved.

Banking paid the bills, but craft beer, ascendant in 1990s San Francisco, became his passion. Sierra Nevada was getting big on the back of its piney flagship pale ale, and Anchor Brewing, led by its easy-drinking Steam beer, grew into a national force. Tremaine loved those sorts of full-flavored beers. He started home-brewing, and one of his first beers, a stout, won second place in a competition. He began nursing dreams of going pro.

Tremaine and two friends from the bank scraped together $5,000 and formed North Beach Brewing with plans to quit their day jobs and make beer. The dreams didn't last long; after half a day at a conference for aspiring brewery owners, it was clear Tremaine and his partners needed far more than $5,000 to build a business. Tremaine stuck with finance.

He moved to Chicago in 1998 to work for LSV Asset Management, a young firm using large data sets to manage $3 billion in assets for large pension funds in the stock market. Tremaine was quickly initiated with his first taste of Jeppson's Malört, at a dive bar one night with a friend. As soon as the bartender learned Tremaine was new to town, he slid a shot across the bar. Tremaine was baffled by what he tasted and, like many people before him, doubly so when he learned it came from Florida.

He didn't think much about Malört for the next decade. Tremaine became chief operating officer at LSV and a partner, which made him eligible for a piece of the profits. The $3 billion the firm managed ballooned to $80 billion—which made Tremaine a wealthy man. He retired before the age of fifty.

He built a sleek five-bedroom, seven-bathroom, fifty-five-hundred-square-foot mansion in one of Chicago's toniest neighborhoods on a piece of land he bought for $1.7 million. Built with an array of materials the architect described as "warm industrial"—lots of metal meeting wood, brick, and concrete—the house featured soaring ceilings, blended indoor-outdoor spaces, and, naturally, a basement bar. Five years later, he sold it for $4.2 million.

For a while, Tremaine was impressed by his own success. Eventually he realized it was a product of luck. Yes, he was smart and he worked hard, but he could just as easily have gone to work for a firm that fizzled out as one that grew as LSV Asset Management had. After sliding into what he would admit was arrogance, he found self-awareness, becoming open about his good fortune and able to laugh sheepishly about the fact that he had made so much money while trying to put it to work in creative and meaningful ways.

When it came time to move on from finance, he wanted to build a business and create jobs. He thought about a platform that allowed rock fans to invest in their favorite independent bands—in essence to own a piece of them while providing the musicians money to tour and record. He considered getting into television production, making a fictional show centered in a Chicago restaurant that followed the lives of a handful of characters. Finally, as craft beer enjoyed a twenty-first-century revival after a decade of stagnation, he thought he might follow through on his early plan to open a brewery. An hour later he was struck with an even better idea: Chicago was already so full of breweries, why not open a distillery?

He knew that many young businesses, especially in the volatile alcohol industry, could be doomed by a lack of capital. That wouldn't be a problem for Tremaine.

———

Pat always figured she'd run Malört as long as she could, maybe even until she died, just as George did. It turned out that by seventy-four, she was ready to be done.

She operated the company for nearly twenty years, the first half listlessly and alone. The second half was a fun, wild sprint filled with new relationships and unlikely adventures. Malört became a rocket ship, something George never experienced during his five decades with the brand. That joy, and the year-after-year sales records that followed, belonged to Pat.

In 2014, the first full year after Peter and Chris left, Malört saw another record-setting sales bump, from 4,584 cases in 2013 to 5,617 in 2014. Surging interest meant she could raise prices to her distributors for the second time in three years—from ninety dollars a case to ninety-four dollars—after not taking a price increase for the eight years prior.

Sales stayed relatively flat in 2015—5,803 cases—which made Pat think the good times had peaked and, once again, Malört's good fortune couldn't last. Then, another burst: more than eight thousand cases sold in 2016 on the way to surpassing ten thousand cases in 2017.

Ten thousand cases! Of Jeppson's Malört! It was nearly a thousand percent growth from a decade earlier.

Chicago remained Malört's core, but small shipments began heading to the pockets of Louisiana, Maryland, Indiana, and Texas that embraced the spirits and cocktail revolution. The growth didn't come easy to Pat's conservative nature, but she finally accepted that Malört's audience was not only real, but real enough to exist beyond Chicago. Requests eventually surpassed the ability to expand. States like Tennessee, where a distributor emailed to say an increasing number of Chicago transplants were asking for Jeppson's Malört, would just have to wait.

The expansion was just a fraction of the total sales but still a radical development for a company approaching growth so cautiously for so long. The paperwork alone exhausted Pat—preparing monthly reports of bottles shipped and bottles sold for each state. There was no one else to handle it.

What Peter and Chris tried convincing her of a few years earlier was finally, undeniably true: she needed more people. There was no other choice. Yet she *still* didn't want to make the investment. Pat didn't like managing one employee, and she certainly didn't want to manage more. Growing a business wasn't the reason she was in business. It was left to her. She had done her job.

Pat didn't want the hassle and she didn't need it. Surging sales and her practice of paying herself the profits at the end of each year pushed her salary from just over $30,000 a few years earlier to more than $400,000. Her financial worries were over, especially considering the value of the

brand itself—from nearly worthless when George died to who knew
how much?

It was time to sell. It was time to rest.

The cold-callers over the years were never serious options; the interest
was no doubt sincere, but so was the likelihood they were hoping to
buy low from the accidental owner of a strange, novel liquor brand. Pat
could spin the company into the world of investment bankers and cash
out with the highest bidder, but that seemed an inappropriate end to
the story that ran from Carl Jeppson to George Brode to her. Besides,
there were already interested parties.

For more than a year, Sam wanted to buy the company. He would
have been a perfect steward to carry it on, a twenty-first-century heir to
George's logic-defying, zany love for Malört. He told Pat his plan: he
would bring production back to Illinois, then after five or ten years of
growing sales, he'd build a place of his own to manufacture Malört in the
heart of Chicago once again. Pat wanted to sell the company to him and
said that if he could raise the money, it would be his. Sam spent months
soliciting family and friends as investors—he just couldn't do it. And Pat
wasn't willing to wait. George kept it until the end partly because it was
his passion, but also because there was nowhere else for it to go. It was
a different world for Malört now. Pat had options.

One of them would have no problem finding the money to buy
Jeppson's Malört: Tremaine Atkinson. Pat thought he was nearly as ideal
a fit as Sam. He didn't have Sam's history with the brand, but he was a
small business owner who seemed likely to care for Malört and already had
the ability to bring it home. Bill O'Donaghue told Pat he was confident
Tremaine had plenty of money to get a deal done. If it wasn't going to
be Sam, Tremaine was the next best option.

Even Sam agreed. He and Tremaine were friendly, and Tremaine
clearly respected his work building the brand. Sam would be able to
stay involved and continue being the face of Malört. It would just be
under Tremaine instead of Pat—and Tremaine's pockets and appetite
for growth were far deeper. In fact, it sounded to Sam like a welcome
change from Pat's years of doubt and hesitation.

Tremaine stood beside the CH bottling line in late 2017 when his phone buzzed. It was Sam. Pat was ready to retire, he said. She wanted to sell. Was he interested?

Of course he was—though he couldn't believe what he was hearing.

A few months earlier, Tremaine had finally resigned himself to never taking over production of Malört from Florida Distillers. His operation had grown from a tiny downtown distillery and bar to a fifty-thousand-square-foot production facility two miles south. It was a $12 million project—nearly $4 million for the two and a half acres of land alone—to build the city's largest distillery, including seventy-five tons of grain storage and a distillation column as tall as a four-story building. In his office hung an 1857 map with an aerial view of Chicago that he bought at auction, one of four known to exist, and the only one in private hands. It was projected to sell for about $25,000, which Tremaine didn't mind paying for a handsome and rare piece of Chicago history. As a bidding war unfolded, Tremaine surprised himself by just how much he wanted the map, sticking with the fevered back-and-forth all the way to $198,600. He didn't regret it for a minute.

The new distillery made him think he could *finally* win Pat's business. Sam told him, with Pat's blessing, what she paid Florida Distillers, and Tremaine undercut the price to make saying no even harder.

Pat still said no. So Tremaine gave up. But now here she was, offering more than the chance to make Malört. He could buy the whole damn thing.

After a few months of due diligence and exchanging information, Tremaine agreed to meet with Pat in Bill O'Donaghue's office on a cool spring morning in 2018. Tremaine was eager to forge a connection and make his case to get a deal done. Instead, he showed up and was surprised to learn Pat would not be there. A day earlier, she told Bill the prospect of a sale felt too raw. She'd leave it to him to speak for her.

"I want to avoid the back and forth and emotional outbursts that a face-to-face meeting might produce," she said. "At least from me."

It was fine with Bill. If anything, it allowed him to speak more openly on behalf of a client like no other.

The one thing she counseled was price. No less than $2 million, she said. Ideally more. She would not, "under any circumstances," take less.

"All in cash, all at once," she said.

She had the figure in mind for more than a year, hashed out with her tax attorney after it became clear Malört's fortunes were irreversibly changed. Sales were at about eight thousand cases at the time. Now they were past ten thousand. She wondered if she could get $2.5 million.

Bill told Tremaine that Pat wasn't there because she wasn't a typical client. And this wouldn't be a standard deal. It couldn't be about bruising negotiation to get to the best price. Tremaine would need to be flexible. Pat needed to feel comfortable. If she felt backed into a corner or he became intractable, the deal wouldn't happen. Play fair and play it straight, Bill said.

Tremaine had guessed as much. It was why he never made a move to buy the company, even as he suspected others did. It never seemed appropriate. He told Bill he had the desire and the ability to do what needed to be done. He passed a letter across the desk with an offer: $1.8 million.

Bill said it wasn't enough, and Tremaine didn't hesitate to up his offer to $2 million. He was surprised when Bill came back with a take-it-or-leave-it figure: $2.2 million. Pat thought the business was worth it.

So did Tremaine, but he said he needed to think about it. Two weeks passed. It was the longest, quietest period of the negotiation. Pat worried the deal might fall apart, but Tremaine was always going to accept. From the moment he sat down in Bill's office, he was going to accept.

The fact was, he wanted Malört, and he wanted it for a simple reason: it was Malört. It was living history—a bitter, yellow-green version of the map hanging on his office wall. It was a brand that defied marketing without much, if any, direct competition; there were other shots, yes, but nothing with the same cachet or affection. Creating such things was nearly impossible, and opportunities to buy them were even rarer than the face that didn't twist up at a first taste of Malört.

It also made perfect business sense. Sales trended in the right direction for six years as a one-and-a-half-person company. Tremaine couldn't imagine what a proper sales effort might yield. He did think he'd be able to get it for $2 million, but the extra $200,000 didn't bother him. He respected Pat's history with Malört and her attachment to it. This was her payday.

CH couldn't have afforded the acquisition on its own, but Tremaine was able to give his company what it needed to finish the deal. His lawyer asked if he was sure. He'd gone up more than 20 percent and nearly $500,000 from his initial offer. Yes, he was sure.

On a Sunday night in late May, Tremaine's lawyer sent Bill an email. Tremaine accepted. He would buy ninety-five cases of Malört, nearly five thousand pounds of wormwood, and Chicago's most iconic liquor brand.

Tremaine was on vacation in Tahiti with his girlfriend, Jennifer, when the deal closed in late September. That night Jennifer, who would soon become Tremaine's second wife, surprised him with dinner on the patio behind their cottage to celebrate the fact that Jeppson's Malört was his. She knew how much he wanted it.

Ten days later, when Tremaine was back in Chicago, they finally announced the deal, breaking the news in the *Chicago Tribune*. A business reporter called Tremaine with an obvious first question: Why did he want to buy Malört?

The answer was at once profound and obvious. "Oh my gosh, why not?" Tremaine said. "I love everything about it. I hate everything about it. It's such a great iconic Chicago thing. It fits at the psychic level, the business level, and the cultural level."

In other words, he understood it.

Even in the mockery of Malört, he said, "there's always an element of love."

"Even if it's ninety percent hate, there's at least ten percent love because it's just so Chicago."

Tremaine said he was already thinking about expanding distribution to forward-thinking markets such as Seattle and Austin, Texas, while remaining true to the brand's history. There would be no expensive or ambitious marketing campaigns. Malört would continue to be Malört. "We're so happy that Pat was willing to give us an opportunity to caretake the brand, and we're not going to mess it up," he said.

Next the reporter called Pat. She struck a wistful tone.

"My entire identity has been Malört for the past 20 years," she said. "Malört was my life. And now it's gone."

For years after George died, and even into the early days of Malört's surge into the mainstream, it still felt like his. Pat was merely the caretaker. Now that the world cared, it felt like hers. Because *she* was the one who did it.

She survived the thujone scare. She toured bars with Mike Sula and chatted with starry-eyed fans. She stared down local distillers using the word *Malört* and fought off mighty Sazerac. She navigated working with lawyers, importers, and Florida Distillers. She brought on Peter Strom, Chris Depa, and Sam Mechling, each of whom helped move the company forward.

Her company.

Now it was hers no longer.

A few weeks later, Tremaine hosted a celebratory dinner at one of Chicago's legendary restaurants, Shaw's Crab House, on a side street tucked between pockets of downtown hubbub. They sat in one of the broad, round booths: Tremaine, Bill, Sam, and a handful of CH employees. Pat initially agreed to join; she and George loved Shaw's. The day before, she changed her mind. She didn't offer an explanation and could barely explain it to herself. She just didn't want to be there. Tremaine was disappointed. Everyone was disappointed. They understood, though.

Fifty-two years earlier Pat walked into George Brode's office. Life flew by—the years of adventure with George, the quiet years without him, the bewildering early days of running Malört on her own, the thrill of the world waking up to it. As she slowly transferred the company to Tremaine—passing off the distributors, the relationships at Florida Distillers, even the wormwood importer—she could scarcely believe it was happening. Now that it was over, it was a moment to mourn as much as celebrate.

She wasn't bitter. It was just bittersweet.

EPILOGUE

TREMAINE ATKINSON THOUGHT of owning Jeppson's Malört like raising kids.

"The best thing you can do," he told an interviewer in 2022, "is not fuck 'em up."

And so it was for Malört. He had used his personal wealth and second career to buy something no company could create, a product with decades of authenticity and (mostly) goodwill that meant different things to different people, for not only its taste but also the memories and emotions it elicited. Tremaine found that fascinating.

He knew Malört was remarkably strong but, in his hands, also fragile. Try to make it something it wasn't, and its momentum could easily derail. He therefore vowed to change little. He kept the ordinary bottle. The cheap, plastic gold-beige cap. Certainly the label. It was inarguably dated, but that was its power. If dozens, or even hundreds, of people tattooed it to their skin, why mess with it? And absolutely, undeniably above all, Malört had to remain the stuff of bitter legend.

As soon as the deal closed, Tremaine began transferring production from Florida Distillers back to Chicago, where Malört would be made for the first time since the Mar-Salle days thirty-three years earlier. There wasn't some grand tome of knowledge to pass down; Florida Distillers simply sent a two-page PDF, the process typed out in fourteen steps no more detailed than baking a batch of brownies. Tremaine tried replicating it, but it came out all wrong—a problem because suddenly the clock was ticking. He had expected five thousand cases of Malört on hand at the time of the sale to last about six months, which would have aligned with recent sales trends. After news of the deal boosted interest, those five thousand cases were on pace to disappear in about half the time.

Most other work at CH was pushed aside as Tremaine and his team churned through test batch after test batch, seeking not only to replicate Jeppson's Malört but to make it better. That didn't mean *tastier*. Instead, Tremaine wanted to build out the front end of the sip, which in truth wasn't bad: grassy and herbal, with notes of grapefruit and honey. Amplifying that first moment would make for an even more dynamic counterpoint in the finish.

They made more than fifty batches, pulling every lever in every direction, though in truth there weren't many levers to pull—just neutral base spirit, wormwood, and sugar. With so few ingredients, minute changes had an outsize impact. He and his team sipped every new attempt, rolling it on the palate, cataloging every flavor, naming every nuance. Eventually they realized that wasn't how people drank Malört. They needed to take shots. That was the only way to judge.

On a snowy Monday morning in early 2019, they finally settled on a passable first batch, then trudged off to celebrate with a dim sum lunch in nearby Chinatown. After returning to the distillery, they tasted it again and affirmed, yup, it was good. They had their Malört.

Weeks later they invited bartenders and bar owners from twenty-five top accounts to visit the distillery for a first taste. Everyone stood around nodding, agreeing it tasted fine, just fine. Some people described it as smooth. Tremaine's stomach dropped; Malört was not meant to be smooth. He realized he had scaled up the test batch with too much sugar, resulting in what one veteran bartender (who, naturally, had a Malört tattoo) described as tasting like "a flat can of Coke you left out all night, but Malört." Tremaine hesitantly sent that batch into the market—better than the market running dry, he thought. Fortunately, it was an easy fix, and the next batch returned Malört to its gritty glory.

With the recipe locked in, Tremaine began chasing all the opportunities that made buying Malört not only a cultural coup but also a savvy business decision. He didn't want to change what Pat—and really, Sam—had built in recent years. He just wanted to do more of it.

He started by boosting Malört's presence in the bars with a flood of tin signs, neon signs, rubber bar mats, and posters bearing the self-effacing slogans of recent years: "Tonight's the night you fight your dad," "When you need to unfriend someone . . . in person," and the like.

Next he turned a modest line of Malört merchandise into an entire genre of Malört *stuff*: flannel shirts, sweatshirts, sports jerseys, swimsuits, socks, shorts, loud Christmas sweaters, a windbreaker, baseball caps, winter hats, a bucket hat, even a seventy-five-dollar adult onesie. There were dog toys, cat toys, a dog hoodie, a pool float, a guitar strap, golf balls, posters, poker chips, a card game, and Christmas ornaments—though nothing ever outsold the T-shirts.

Then Tremaine began doing the things Pat couldn't or wouldn't. He invested close to $100,000 to package Malört in fifty-milliliter plastic bottles, the ones found on airplanes, which he sold in six-packs. The tiny bottles seemed an ideal vessel for gifting, tailgating, and, naturally, traveling; Tremaine always stuck a couple six-packs in his suitcase to introduce Malört to people on the road. They became about 10 percent of the business.

He teamed with one of Chicago's buzziest local craft breweries, Marz Community Brewing, to create Malört Spritz, a canned cocktail layering Malört with grapefruit soda, hibiscus, and lime juice to a "balanced, citrusy" conclusion with "pleasingly bitter grapefruit flavor," one reviewer said. It was a small project, but it helped affirm Malört's credibility in Chicago's craft community.

When a bourbon under the CH banner didn't sell well, Tremaine tried again using Carl Jeppson's name. Jeppson's Bourbon was the first new "Jeppson's" product since Malört and initially bore a similar label in a tweaked color scheme. It garnered initial interest but also confusion: Was Malört in this bourbon? It was not, but when sales plateaued after eighteen months, Tremaine changed the label to a cleaner, more modern look. Jeppson's Bourbon was no juggernaut, but sales again began climbing.

The real opportunity lay simply in expanding Malört's footprint. When out-of-state distributors started vying for Pat's attention in 2012, she hesitantly pushed small amounts into a few states—five of them by the time Tremaine bought the brand. That was as much as she could stand. Growth scared and exhausted Pat. Tremaine craved it.

Early on it came easy. Pent-up demand had distributors coming to him, and he was willing to ship to any state where he was shown a smart sales and marketing plan. Once that interest slowed, Tremaine's salesforce of seven people started pushing more aggressively—the kind of effort Peter and Chris had envisioned—until Malört was sold in thirty states plus Washington, DC. It became CH's largest brand, accounting for 65 percent of production.

Chicago remained the core, but by 2024 Malört was also sold on the West Coast and the East Coast, in mountain states and plains states, across the Midwest and in the South. Chicago accounted for more than 90 percent of sales when Tremaine bought the brand. Five years later Chicago was less than 60 percent, though more was sold in the city than at the time of the sale.

The strongest markets beyond Chicago were hearty Midwestern states close to home (Wisconsin, Indiana, and Minnesota) and western cities with decades of progressive drinking culture (Denver, Austin, Seattle, and Portland). Malört didn't connect with every new audience. So many ex-Chicagoans lived in Arizona that the CH sales team figured Malört must do well there. Maybe it was the heat or the demographics, but it didn't.

It did resonate in some unique and surprising pockets. Pepp's Pub, just beyond New Orleans's French Quarter, launched what it called Malortigras in 2021, an annual late-July celebration of Malört-themed songs, frozen Malört cocktails, and three-dollar Malört shots. Pepp's could plow through nearly a hundred bottles during the five-hour event, though in reality Pepp's celebrated Malört year round.

Its owner, Sam Wurth, discovered Malört as a bartender in Chicago a decade earlier and was initially infuriated after coworkers slipped it in as an initiation rite when he expected the shot of Jameson he'd asked for. Once he calmed, he was intrigued. Soon he was an ardent fan. At Pepp's he indoctrinated customers with half-ounce samples, snapping Polaroids of their reactions and having them write descriptions of what they tasted at the bottom of the photos in black marker (highlights included "Bitter fart," "Bigfoot's dick," and "FUCK!!"). Sam wallpapered the bar's bathroom walls with the photos.

Malört on tap, once a radical proposition, became increasingly common across Chicago and migrated to bars beyond—in Seattle; St. Louis; Fayetteville, Arkansas; and more. Malört even earned a category in a Denver alt-weekly newspaper's annual best-of issue—"Best Place to Drink Malört"—an honor given to a bar whose menu a thousand miles from Chicago included the Chicago Handshake.

———————

The pandemic was painful. Bars and restaurants across Illinois closed at 9:00 PM on March 16, 2020, for what turned out to be nearly three months, then spent the next year opening and closing. With the pandemic went half of Malört's sales.

Tremaine didn't fret. He even had some fun with the moment, distilling more than fourteen hundred kegs of India pale ale from Chicago's Revolution Brewing into the first-ever Jeppson's Malört made from beer. Emptying each keg by hand was arduous, but with the world largely at a standstill and the beer about to go out of code thanks to the shutdown, CH had plenty of time for creative larks. The result was an even huskier take on Malört.

As hand sanitizer became essential during the early days of COVID-19, dozens of distilleries aided the effort by blending neutral grain spirit, glycerin, and hydrogen peroxide. CH was among them, introducing what Tremaine called Malört Hand Sanitizer, given free to first responders and health care workers. The label featured Malört's signature crest and riffed on George Brode's old line about "two-fisted drinkers." Malört Hand Sanitizer, the label said, offered "two-fisted clean."

"Everyone needs a little bit of a laugh and something to make them smile," Tremaine told the *Chicago Tribune* two weeks into the pandemic. "We know how people feel about Malört, so we figured why not throw the name on."

In 2021, as the world inched back to normalcy, Malört recovered its lost pandemic sales. In 2022, as bars fully reopened and patrons were thrilled to be back out, it surged. In 2023 it grew again, especially beyond Illinois. By 2024 it sold more than thirty thousand cases, stunning heights for a brand that could have disappeared twenty years earlier with hardly anyone noticing.

So, no. Tremaine didn't fuck up Jeppson's Malört. Though owning something so many people felt ownership of could get tricky.

Some longtime Malört fans insisted they preferred Florida Distillers' version to CH's update for being more ragged at the edges and therefore more authentically Malört. Scofflaw kept it on tap, but its sales slowed as the brand transitioned from hipster calling card to mainstream ubiquity (the inevitable next step after the transition from old-man shot to hipster calling card).

Even Wyl Villacres, winner of Sam's tattoo contest, considered having his prize covered up. His affinity for Malört dimmed as its popularity grew, plus he'd become a dad; did he really want a liquor brand inked on his arm?

The biggest crisis came in late 2023, when Tremaine and his team borrowed an idea from a handful of bars, including longtime ally Nisei Lounge, which had infused Malört with other flavors for close to a decade, from coffee to Skittles to sport peppers. CH released a pumpkin spice Malört that October. In November it sought to mimic Thanksgiving flavors by infusing turkey bouillon, cranberry, and sage. The plan for December was to rest Malört on fir tips, to add hints of resin and citrus to the familiar bitterness. When the fir-tip supplier failed to come through at the last minute, CH pivoted to the easiest Christmas flavor it could think of: candy canes.

Bottles of each infusion cost $150, generating nearly $100,000 for three charities. Chicago media, which couldn't get enough of Malört, feverishly covered each new release—though the last round brought more attention than Tremaine wanted.

Two hours after CH announced its candy cane version, Nisei Lounge unfurled months of pent-up rage, saying on social media it had "sat quietly while you built your brand this fall copying our infusions and selling them as house bottles at CH at a filthy profit without crediting us." A candy cane Malört was an infusion too far.

"THIS IS FUCKING BULLSHIT," Nisei wrote. "Quit stealing our mixology ideas without attribution."

CH publicly apologized a day later with a statement drafted by Tremaine, addressed to "all the bartenders, bars, and other good folks who are OG originators of infused Malört."

"In our rush to do good," Tremaine wrote, "we missed acknowledging those who came before us in the quest to make Malört worse."

The social media critics were unmoved, noting the apology still failed to credit Nisei Lounge as originator of candy cane Malört. Nisei, too, persisted in its grievance, renaming its longtime favorite shot "Chicago non-apology apology juice" and referring to it as "M*****" on social media. Soon T-shirts emerged ("Nisei Lounge infused Malört first"), and Nisei hung a vinyl banner outside the bar made hastily with stencils and red spray paint:

CANDY CANE
MALORT
BORN HERE 2016

Staff debated whether to pull out of a Chicago Handshake bar crawl in the coming months but voted to remain. Explaining why one of Chicago's quintessential Malört accounts wasn't taking part would have been exhausting. Instead, Nisei's punishment was more low-key: it stopped promoting Malört on its well-read social media channels.

Tremaine was surprised by the depth of the blowback. He was disappointed too. Malört was meant to unite, not divide. And it wasn't as if Nisei was the only bar to infuse Malört. He knew of at least two or three others. But the episode underscored a truth about Malört, and it was much of what led him to spend more than $2 million for it.

It wasn't just a bitter gag. People felt it innately.

———————

Sam was initially along for the ride. It didn't last long. Once he couldn't raise the money to buy Malört or even to partner with Tremaine, it became Tremaine's deal alone. Sam was disappointed but also a proponent. A sale to Tremaine would be the best thing for Pat, who could finally retire, and for Malört, which would be made in Chicago again. Things were occasionally awkward between Sam and Tremaine, but everyone agreed they were headed for the right outcome.

Instead of a partner, Sam agreed to come on as a CH employee. They just never quite figured out his role. He started as the seasonal Malört merch crush was taking off and spent his early days packing, labeling, and mailing boxes. He did one marketing event, at a rock festival just before Christmas 2018, posing for photos as a disheveled Santa Claus nursing a bottle of Malört.

Sam otherwise felt he was put to strangely little use. He wasn't part of the team trying to reproduce Malört after taking over production from Florida Distillers. He took that as a slight. Who understood the taste of Malört better than him? Finally, he was assigned to the sales team, told that was where he was needed. He made a few calls but never took to the job.

Sam's talent was to amuse and surprise, thriving with the freedom someone like Pat offered, even if it sometimes came grudgingly. Pat hated being a boss, and all she asked of Sam was a weekly email detailing where he went, who he saw, and what he sold. One week he'd send the email, the next few he'd skip until Pat badgered him into doing it again. Then he'd send the email, stop again, and the process began anew. Pat finally gave up. Sometimes Sam didn't even respond to her emails. What was Pat really going to do about it? They both knew the answer.

Tremaine offered no such latitude. He was no accidental business owner. He had goals. He held his people to high standards. Fair standards, he thought. But high. He demanded accountability and basic benchmarks of success. For a salesperson, that was not only selling but also organization, accountability, communication, and commitment.

At the end of 2018 Tremaine pulled Sam aside and said it was over. He said he was appreciative of their friendship and how the deal came together, but that it was time to move on. He offered $50,000, insisting it wasn't severance but a finder's fee for facilitating the sale.

Sam knew things weren't going well, but no longer preaching Malört's gospel, and losing the thing he loved like a person, it hurt like a breakup. It *was* a breakup. He thought of Peter Strom. Suddenly, he understood.

He and Tremaine stayed on OK terms. He even came back weeks later for the big reveal of the first taste. He was conflicted, but everyone agreed it would be weirder for him not to be there. When Tremaine had a question about Malört's history or how to stage an event, he kept calling on Sam. In interviews Tremaine continued touting Sam's role building the brand: "His love for Malört is contagious," he said in a 2023 interview.

When asked over the years why he no longer worked for Malört, Sam turned stoic and philosophical, saying the time had come to move on. Though he remained friendly with Tremaine, he told a radio interviewer in 2023, once it was clear he "wouldn't be able to kind of continue my role as directly with the brand . . . it just no longer made sense" to remain at CH.

"It's like raising a kid," he said. "Eventually you kind of have to let them go on their own."

It may have been somewhat true. Even so, it hurt. For years it hurt.

Months after leaving CH, Sam took a job as a salesman at a Chicago craft beer distributor. A few months later came the pandemic, which changed everything. Much of his network left the industry or moved away. Everything felt different.

In 2021 he moved with his girlfriend to Columbus to be closer to family. It took two years, but he finally registered his car in Ohio, sending his beloved "MALORT" license plate back into the Illinois wilderness.

———————

Pat never talked to Peter or Chris again.

She would remember Chris as helpful and good at what he did, Peter as enthusiastic and "a sweet young man." Always he was "a sweet young man." In the end, they asked too much. She didn't begrudge them for asking. They were right that she needed to invest in the company—hindsight made it clear. She just wasn't ever going to be the one to do it. It wasn't her way. She had no regrets.

Pat only spoke to Sam a few more times. The last was in 2020, in the early days of the pandemic. He was updating his résumé and wanted to chart Malört's growth while he was with the company. Pat happily supplied annual sales figures but didn't hear from him again. She felt bad—bad that she didn't sell the company to him and bad that he didn't last at CH. She'd wonder for years if she could have done things differently, could have done them better. She missed Sam.

In the second half of her seventies, having ever owned Malört grew dimmer and dimmer. A man in her building emailed to say he saw something on the news about the Chicago Handshake. Pat had to look it up on the internet to remember what it was. She never really cared about that stuff.

Sometimes she'd see something on TV—like singer turned talk show host Kelly Clarkson making news in early 2023 by trying Malört on her show and declaring, "That's good!"—and it would all come rushing back.

Oh my God! There's Malört!

Dueling feelings always came. Pat was glad to see the brand stronger than ever, and to know she'd done her part to make it happen. That felt good. But she was disappointed George didn't see any of it, and she was wistful Malört wasn't hers anymore. Owning it made for some of the most thrilling days of her life. Certainly not the early years, as sales fell and she navigated the thujone scare. And she didn't miss the stress, the uncertainty, or the paperwork.

Once Mike Sula clued her in to how modern tastes embraced Malört, and then Peter, Chris, and Sam came into her life and her business, Malört was a thrilling ride at a time most women her age were playing cards or reveling in grandchildren. She was meeting people and passing fun, late nights in bars.

Pat never dreamed she'd get the money she did for Jeppson's Malört, though it didn't feel like some grand conquest. She wouldn't even remember exactly how much she got for the business. She thought that was kind of funny; most people would remember the details of something so life changing. It was never really about the money, just the comfort of knowing she would always be comfortable. She'd never had that.

If the sale had happened a decade earlier, Pat thought, she might have bought a little cottage in southwest Michigan, the peaceful respite from city life she and George enjoyed every summer for years. She'd never been until meeting him, and on her first visit, she felt like she was meant to be there. She loved browsing the shops and watching the boats in the harbor and midnight swims at the hotel pool. She was never more relaxed or carefree. A place there of her own would have been a dream. It seemed too late for that now.

Instead, she spent quiet days alone in the condo, passing the time with movies and bad TV, getting out for groceries or to get her hair done. As George aged, she so dearly wanted to live in his condo. Back then she was dazzled by the twenty-fourth-floor views of the lake. Now there were days she didn't even see it.

In early 2023 Tremaine finally tired of the whole Malört face thing. He had enough of mocking Jeppson's Malört and the lamentations of how bad it was. It was time for a new message, a new bridge to the world. Because it *wasn't* bad. Sure, part of the fun was moaning about the bitterness, but if it wasn't respected and appreciated, business wouldn't have grown as it did. It was time for something else. He spent six months weighing the options.

There was a potential "better for you" approach. Malört was as low in sugar as liqueur got, hence the intense bitterness. Most others, especially the fruitiest ones, were loaded with sugar and calories, the trade-off for tasting "good."

It also had an interesting cultural history—the angle Peter Strom championed before departing nearly ten years earlier. Tremaine visited Sweden for a couple days in 2022 to attend a wormwood harvest and to learn more about besk's place in Swedish culture. He met twenty-five people from Ystad—Carl Jeppson's hometown—and tried ten different besks. He was surprised to find that besk was made by regular people, often with their own twists and ample senses of pride. He wondered if he might position Malört as a one-of-a-kind, and maybe even vaguely sophisticated, European-style product, rooted in its Swedish heritage.

He also considered borrowing George Brode's old approach from the 1960s, painting Malört as a drink for the tough, the renegades, the fighters. Tremaine would drop the '60s-era machismo ("Are you man enough to drink Jeppson?"), but articulating Malört's brashness as something for the brave, rather than as the eternal butt of the joke, could be just enough to update the narrative.

Then he realized none of it made sense. What people liked to talk about was the bitterness, the difficulty, and the fact they couldn't stand it (even when they loved not being able to stand it). Lamenting Malört was just as much the point as drinking it. So he didn't change a thing. In 2024 he launched a marketing campaign doubling down on what he knew worked, rooted in sharing and celebrating Malört faces on social media.

The credit went to an unlikely source: the rapper and singer Drake. In July 2023, while in Chicago to play a pair of shows at a sports arena, the Toronto native posted a dim photo of a Malört bottle on his Instagram feed, taken in the candlelit bar of a high-end downtown sushi restaurant. He'd just taken a first taste at a bartender's urging as a "true Chicago experience."

Drake was a good sport about it, but couldn't believe what he tasted. His caption to his 140 million followers: "There's no way Chicago enjoys this . . ."

Media, of course, pounced. It was one of the world's biggest music stars! Hating Malört!

DRAKE HAD THE AUDACITY TO SHIT TALK MALORT WHILE IN CHICAGO, read one headline.

DRAKE THINKS HE'S TOO GOOD FOR MALÖRT, read another.

A Reddit thread sprang up about the news. The title: "Even Drake Hates Malört." (One reply said it was the "most real shit Drake has said in his whole career.")

Overnight, Tremaine's biggest brand got countless impressions and the equivalent of hundreds of thousands of dollars in free advertising. That alone, though, didn't convince him to stand pat. As he scrolled through the replies to Drake's post, he realized this was the conversation people craved. They wanted to trash-talk Malört and to pick on it (or, conversely, to defend it). Its punch-line status resonated—still. So he left it alone.

What he did update in early 2024 was the bottle, both to honor Malört's history and so that it no longer quite "screamed cheap," as Peter and Chris once said. Tremaine wouldn't have attempted such a change until owning Malört at least a few years, but it felt like enough time had passed that he could do it credibly.

The bottle was custom made, nodding to how George Brode packaged Malört in the 1950s and '60s, with more graceful curves and the words CARL JEPPSON CO., CHICAGO USA embossed around the neck. Out went the cheap gold-beige plastic cap and paper neck label, replaced by a brown metal cap connected to a metal neck band. Tremaine restored the back label to George's old black-and-white design and, of course, left the front label untouched.

The most subtle tweak sat on the bottom of the bottle. It was there without explanation, just a tiny nugget for Malört fans to pursue if they wished.

It was four sets of initials:

CJ
GB
PG
CH

ACKNOWLEDGMENTS

THANK YOU TO Pat Gabelick, who I called on a Saturday afternoon in January 2022 to explain my idea of writing the story of Jeppson's Malört. The call went to her answering machine. As I babbled into it, she picked up the phone. We started talking and didn't stop for more than two years. She was endlessly good natured and open, wondering what else I could possibly ask, then continuing to explain the details of a life she seemed to find ordinary but that I found extraordinary. She told me many times I was welcome to write anything we discussed, and she stuck to it.

Thank you to the people who made both the rise of Malört and this book possible: in the order they entered the story, Peter Strom, Chris Depa, and Sam Mechling. Each was patient, kind, and generous, discussing the good times and the bad openly and honestly. Extra thanks to Peter for doing so much work to assemble the history of Jeppson's Malört before I ever started digging into it, then acting as a sounding board as I tried to make sense of it. Many thanks also to Tremaine Atkinson for his time and candor.

Thanks for help along the way from Michael and Karen Riddet; the Skokie Public Library and Joshua Mabe at the Chicago Public Library; Kevin Leonard at Northwestern University; Mike Sula at the *Chicago Reader*; the bartenders at Miru for giving Drake that shot; Ryan Ori; Ashley Brandt; Leo Belleville and Stephen Spence at the National Archives; and Dan and Abby Healy, who shared the Green Mill anecdote. Thank you also to Rachel Dickens and Adam Collins for the support and encouragement.

Thanks to Alice Speilburg; Kara Rota, Jerome Pohlen, Devon Freeny and everyone at Chicago Review Press; Joe Gray; Ira Berkow; Michael Hawthorne; Brett Nolan, once again, for honest and helpful feedback; David MacLean, for the last-minute writing consultation; Alex Parker, for catching the typo; Meahgan Miller; John and Anne Lavelle; and the many friends and teachers along the way.

Above all, thanks to my family: Stacie Geller and Jonathan Frenzen; Howard, Rhoda, and Gabriel Noel; Aunt Carla; Marsha and Bob; Peter, Gloria, Leon, and Lewis; Lauren and our two special people to whom this book is dedicated.

NOTES & SOURCES

Unless otherwise indicated, all quotes are from author interviews or the Malört archives.

NOTES

PROLOGUE

"a forest fire": Matt Moore, "What Does Malört Taste Like? Sun-Times Readers Weigh In," *Chicago Sun-Times*, August 25, 2021, https://chicago.suntimes .com/entertainment-and-culture/2021/8/25/22641237/what-does-malort -taste-like-chicago-liquor.

"burnt vinyl car-seat": John Wilmes, "Chicago's Malört Liqueur Is Both Off-Putting and Excellent," *Food & Wine*, May 12, 2022, https://www .foodandwine.com/travel/history-of-malort-chicago-novelty-liquor.

"hairspray and death": "So, What Does Malort Taste Like?," Reddit, November 10, 2011, https://www.reddit.com/r/chicago/comments/m7qmq/so_what _does_malort_taste_like/.

"swallowing a burnt condom": *Drinking Buddies*, directed by Joe Swanberg (Magnolia Pictures, 2013).

"pencil shavings and heartbreak": "John Hodgman," episode 354 of *WTF with Marc Maron* (podcast), January 21, 2013, https://www.wtfpod.com/podcast /episodes/episode_354_-_john_hodgman.

"It's making me grind": Kat Odell, "10 Top New York Sommeliers Try Malört," *Eater*, April 27, 2016, https://www.eater.com/drinks/2016/4/27/11148504 /malort-liqueur-chicago-sommelier-new-york-city.

long wrestled with Malört's allure: Kevin J. Gray, "Malort Is the Worst Booze Ever. And You Need to Try It," *Paste*, February 17, 2016, https://www .pastemagazine.com/drink/malort-is-the-worst-booze-ever-and-you-need -to-try; John Wilmes, "Why This Off-Putting Chicago Novelty Liquor Is So Damn Special," Yahoo Life, https://www.yahoo.com/lifestyle/why-off -putting-chicago-novelty-154332017.html; Sam Greszes, "Malort: Sin Against God or Actually, Kinda Good?," *Thrillist*, August 21, 2016, https:// www.thrillist.com/drink/chicago/jeppsons-malort-chicago-liquor.

"This is actually painful": Odell, "10 Top New York Sommeliers."

1. GEORGE AND PAT

"SECRETARY": Classified advertisement (p. D34), *Chicago Tribune*, January 9, 1966.

"Can a panty-waist drink Jeppson?": Advertisement, *Chicago Tribune*, April 1, 1967.

"Jeppson the two-fisted liquor": Advertisement, *Chicago Tribune*.

"No panty-waist drinker": Advertisement, *Chicago Tribune*, June 17, 1967.

"The streets were freedom": "The Adventures of Saul Bellow," *American Masters*, PBS, December 12, 2022, https://www.pbs.org/video/the-adventures-of -saul-bellow-tswuvt/.

2. A YEAR AND A DAY

"involved several million dollars": "George Broide Buys Interests of Bielzoff Co.," *Chicago Tribune*, July 15, 1945.

"I handle the priorities and maintenance" to *"What makes this more serious"*: United States v. George Broide, accessed February 26, 2022, National Archives, Chicago, IL.

"A wealthy Glencoe resident": "Glencoe Draft Evader Gets Year in Prison," *Chicago Tribune*, May 15, 1947.

"36 story crown jewel": Classified advertisement (pt. 3, p. 8), *Chicago Tribune*, February 16, 1963.

3. THE HORNY-HANDED MALE ARTISAN

"Remember the first time": Courtesy of Pat Gabelick. Subsequent advertisements quoted in this chapter are from the same source.

"We don't believe Jeppson drinkers": Courtesy of Pat Gabelick.

"lots and lots of advertisements": Courtesy of Pat Gabelick.

"Greatest liquor campaign ever": Courtesy of Pat Gabelick.

5. JUST BE PATIENT

"I enjoyed your letter immensely": Courtesy of Michael Riddet.

"10/03/85—Rappin ordered": Courtesy of Pat Gabelick.

6. THEY FOUND IT IN EACH OTHER

"We're talking about carving up": Courtesy of Pat Gabelick.

"damaged his character": Charles Mount, "She Goes to Court for Name's Sake," *Chicago Tribune*, May 14, 1977.

"cattle brand" to *"I'm not cattle"*: "His Name but Hers to Keep," *New York Times*, May 22, 1977, https://www.nytimes.com/1977/05/22/archives/his-name -but-hers-to-keep.html.

"A rose is a rose is a rose": Charles Mount, "She Goes to Court."

7. YET SOMEHOW, THE STRANGE DRINK CALLED JEPPSON'S MALÖRT HAS SURVIVED

"This shit tastes like crap": Patrick Sisson, "An Oral History of the Green Mill," *Chicago Reader*, March 20, 2014, https://chicagoreader.com/music/an-oral -history-of-the-green-mill/.

"the ultimate alcoholic aesthete": Ben McFarland and Tom Sandham, *The Thinking Drinker's Guide to Alcohol: A Cocktail of Amusing Anecdotes and Opinion on the Art of Imbibing* (New York: Sterling Epicure, 2014), 202.

"makers of wine, bitters": Courtesy of Pat Gabelick.

"to the best of our knowledge": Courtesy of Pat Gabelick.

"With storage charges in excess": Courtesy of Pat Gabelick.

"When you breathe it in" to *"the one-person operation"*: Mark Brown, "What Drink Asks 'Are You Man Enough?' It's a Liqueur So Bad—or Wonderful—It's Only Sold Here," *Chicago Sun-Times*, May 6, 2007.

8. WHAT THE FUCK WAS THAT?

"dark, dangerous" and *"drugs, prostitution"*: Robert Simonson, "Milk & Honey, New Year's Eve 1999," Punch, December 31, 2019, https://punchdrink .com/articles/milk-and-honey-cocktail-bar-nyc-new-years-eve-1991/.

"an idiot-free environment": Julia Chaplin, "Buzz Off: Secret Bars That Spurn Hype," *New York Times*, May 7, 2000, https://www.nytimes.com/2000 /05/07/style/buzz-off-secret-bars-that-spurn-hype.html.

"brought cocktails from the penthouse": Robert Simonson, *A Proper Drink: The Untold Story of How a Band of Bartenders Saved the Civilized Drinking World* (Berkeley, CA: Ten Speed Press, 2016), 159.

"1. No name-dropping": John Del Signore, "Milk & Honey, Cocktail Mecca, Goes from Secret to Private," *Gothamist*, October 17, 2008, https://gothamist.com/food/milk-honey-cocktail-mecca-goes-from-secret-to-private.

"If submitting to authority": R G., one-star review of Milk & Honey, Yelp, August 27, 2011, https://www.yelp.com/biz/milk-and-honey-new-york-2?rr=1.

"it just didn't go down": Mike Sula, "Waiting for the Hour," *Chicago Reader*, July 30, 2007, https://chicagoreader.com/blogs/waiting-for-the-hour/.

"a midcourse between sexy": "Empire Liquors," *Time Out Chicago*, February 3, 2014, https://www.timeout.com/chicago/bars/empire-liquors-closed.

9. I HAVE HEARD IT DESCRIBED AS "IF YOU DRANK WATER OUT OF AN ASH TRAY"

"this is a place to post": Malört Face, Instagram, accessed January 9, 2024, https://www.flickr.com/groups/malortface/.

10. PAT GABELICK WALKS INTO A BAR . . .

"prickly old lady": Mike Sula, "Busted!," *Chicago Reader*, November 4, 2004, https://chicagoreader.com/news-politics/busted-4/.

"landscaper named Gustavo": Mike Sula, "The Two-Car Taqueria," *Chicago Reader*, September 3, 2009, https://chicagoreader.com/food-drink/the-two-car-taqueria/.

"I never would have guessed": Mike Sula, "Chicken of the Trees," *Chicago Reader*, August 16, 2012, https://chicagoreader.com/food-drink/chicken-of-the-trees/.

"some of my favorite bartenders" and *"a concerted two-year campaign"*: Mike Sula, "Shot of Malort, Hold the Grimace," *Chicago Reader*, April 9, 2009, https://chicagoreader.com/food-drink/omnivorous-shot-of-malort-hold-the-grimace/.

"They both loved it" to *"I'm hopeful"*: Sula, "Shot of Malort."

"worst liquor in the world": "Peter vs. the Worst Liquor in the World," *Wait Wait . . . Don't Tell Me!*, NPR, June 9, 2011, https://www.npr.org/sections/waitwait/2011/06/09/137080198/peter-vs-the-worst-liquor-in-the-world.

11. PAT AND PETER

"I've really enjoyed your articles": Courtesy of Mike Sula.

"no apparent ill effects": Mike Sula, "Homemade Malort," *Chicago Reader*, April 9, 2009, https://chicagoreader.com/blogs/homemade-malort/.

"Mike Sula forwarded your e-mail": Courtesy of Pat Gabelick.

"There does seem to be": Courtesy of Pat Gabelick.

12. PETER AND CHRIS

"FACT: The wormwood in Malort": https://twitter.com/JeppsonsMalort/status /59425178660245504.

"It is currently 98.6°F": https://twitter.com/JeppsonsMalort/status /93771691850866688.

"When my kid turns 5": https://twitter.com/JeppsonsMalort/status /121660148988129280.

"Spending your time working": Courtesy of Pat Gabelick.

"Chicago businessman George Brode": Courtesy of Pat Gabelick.

"It's the rebirth": Kim Janssen, "3 Local Liquor Makers Revive Once-Thriving Cottage Industry," *Chicago Sun-Times*, December 22, 2011, https://chicago .suntimes.com/news/2011/12/22/18531886/3-local-liquor-makers-revive -once-thriving-cottage-industry.

13. SAM

"Enclosed, please find": Courtesy of Pat Gabelick. Subsequent documents quoted in this chapter are from the same source.

14. I HOPE HE IS WATCHING US

"Believe me, part of me": Courtesy of Pat Gabelick.

"My first tattoo was": Anthony Todd, "The Man with the Malort Tattoo," Chicagoist, August 21, 2012, https://chicagoist.com/2012/08/21/the_man _with_the_malort_tattoo.php.

"I hope he is watching": Mark Peters, "In Chicago, a Spirit Rises Despite Bitter Reviews," *Wall Street Journal*, November 20, 2012, https://www.wsj.com /articles/SB10001424052702303296604577454872180605752.

"awfulness is throwing me" to *"Ms. Gabelick seems a bit baffled"*: Peters, "In Chicago, a Spirit Rises."

15. WHAT IF WE MADE OUR OWN MALÖRT?

"He would have loved this": *This Story Will Never End*, directed by Marc Pearlman (Fire Engine Red Films, 2014).

"The bartenders liked it": Interview with the author, January 21, 2022.

"whiskey-drinking hippie": Mike Sula, "Moonshiner Goes Legit: Letherbee Distillers," *Chicago Reader*, April 27, 2012, https://chicagoreader.com/blogs /moonshiner-goes-legit-letherbee-distillers/.

"free from corporate compromises": "About," Letherbee Distillers, accessed January 9, 2024, https://www.letherbee.com/about.

"The wormwood liqueur's flavor" to *"There's a small contingency"*: Robert Simonson, "Another Taste of Malört Is Arriving in Chicago," *New York Times*, October 12, 2012, https://archive.nytimes.com/dinersjournal.blogs .nytimes.com/2012/10/12/another-taste-of-malort-is-arriving-to-chicago/.

"A Swede would never name": Courtesy of Pat Gabelick.

16. MOVE OVER, MALÖRT

"Violet Hour Malört gives Jeppson's": "Violet Hour Malort Gives Jeppson's High -Class Competition as Cult Status of the Chicago Spirit Grows," *Huffington Post*, January 9, 2013, https://www.huffpost.com/entry/violet-hour-malort -gives_n_2443163.

"Thinking they can do better": Mason Johnson, "The New Malort: The Worst Drink to Ever Happen to Chicago . . . Again," CBS News Chicago, May 31, 2013, https://www.cbsnews.com/chicago/news/the-new-malort-the-worst -drink-to-ever-happen-to-chicago-again/.

"Move over Malort?": Mick Swasko, "Move Over Malort? Chicago Bar to Brew Their Own Beast," *RedEye*, October 15, 2012, https://www.chicagotribune .com/redeye/ct-redeye-xpm-2012-10-15-34477728-story.html.

"truly local": Julia Thiel, "Best Locally Made Malort," *Chicago Reader*, June 19, 2013, https://chicagoreader.com/best-of-chicago/best-locally-made-malort/.

"an almost shockingly bitter": Michell Eloy, "House-Made Malort from Violet Hour," *Chicago Tribune*, January 31, 2013.

smelling like *"rubbing alcohol"*: Emmet Sullivan, "The Power of Malört," *Chicago*, March 27, 2014, https://www.chicagomag.com/chicago-magazine /april-2014/the-power-of-malort/.

"social media-savvy": "Jeppson's Malort's Social Media Misfire," *Crain's Chicago Business*, July 19, 2013, https://www.chicagobusiness.com/article/20130719 /BLOGS08/130719755/jeppson-s-malort-apologizes-for-social-media-misfire.

17. PAT AND SAM

"this sort of dry": Kelly Bauer, "Malort Fan Makes Love for Drink, and Chicago, Permanent with Ink," *DNAinfo*, July 7, 2014, https://www.dnainfo.com /chicago/20140707/west-town/malort-fan-makes-love-for-drink----chicago ----permanent-with-ink/.

"'The Malort Song' Is Archie Powell's": Mick Swasko, "'The Malort Song' Is Archie Powell's Most Bitter Release," *Chicago Tribune*, October 17, 2014.

"It started as a joke": Josh Noel, "Malort Gains Fans as Battle Brews over Name," *Chicago Tribune*, January 15, 2014.

gave Malört to ten: Odell, "10 Top New York Sommeliers."

unsuspecting musical acts: The A.V. Club, "The Flaming Lips, Descendents, Pierce the Veil, and Others Try Shots of Malort," YouTube, October 4, 2016, https://www.youtube.com/watch?v=2XqITJEUrks.

"Without any doubt": Courtesy of Pat Gabelick.

18. AND NOW IT'S GONE

"It tastes like lead": Hunter Hobbs, "Different Countries Try Malort—the Worst Liquor Ever," YouTube, April 9, 2017, https://www.youtube.com /watch?v=1ANDZYAx7tQ.

named Sam's job: Jay Gentile, "11 Cool Chicago Jobs You'd Take in a Heartbeat," *Thrillist*, https://www.thrillist.com/amphtml/lifestyle/chicago/the-11-coolest -jobs-in-chicago.

"the heart and soul": "Sam Mechling of Jeppson's Malort," episode 67 of *Good Beer Hunting* (podcast), January 23, 2016, https://www.goodbeerhunting .com/gbh-podcast/2016/1/13/ep-067-sam-mechling-of-jeppsons-malort.

finally announced the deal: Greg Trotter, "Pilsen Distillery Acquires Malort, Aims to Bring Production of the Bitter Liquor Back to Chicago," *Chicago Tribune*, October 5, 2018.

EPILOGUE

"The best thing": Charles Awad and Ben Quam, "Squatter by Association with Malört's Tremaine Atkinson," episode 54 of *Libations for Everyone* (podcast), June 21, 2022, https://rss.com/podcasts/libationsforeveryone/526889/.

"balanced, citrusy": Malört Spritz review, Tastings.com, accessed February 1, 2024, https://www.tastings.com/Spirits-Review/Jeppsons-Malort-Spritz -RTD-USA-12-oz-02-01-2021.aspx.

annual best-of issue: "Best Place to Drink Malört," *Westword*, accessed February 23, 2024, https://www.westword.com/best-of/2022/food-and-drink/best -place-to-drink-malort-13810925.

"Everyone needs a little bit": Josh Noel, "Coronavirus Pandemic Produces the Inevitable for Chicago: Malort Hand Sanitizer," *Chicago Tribune*, March 24, 2020.

mimic Thanksgiving flavors: Jeppson's Malört (@JeppsonsMalort), "NEW LIMITED EDITION MALÖRT DROP . . . ," Twitter, November 1, 2023, https://twitter.com/JeppsonsMalort/status/1719850064326095095.

"sat quietly while you built": Nisei Lounge Chicago (@NiseiLounge), "Look @ JeppsonsMalort we've sat quietly . . . ," Twitter, December 1, 2023, https:// twitter.com/NiseiLounge/status/1730764211750355189.

"all the bartenders": Jeppson's Malört (@JeppsonsMalort), "SORRY . . . ," Twitter, December 2, 2023, https://twitter.com/JeppsonsMalort/status /1731009854536335563.

"Chicago non-apology": Monocle Man (@MonocleMan1), "Undisclosed location . . . ," Twitter, December 20, 2023, https://twitter.com /MonocleMan1/status/1737642674432434222/photo/3.

"wouldn't be able to": Adriana Cardona-Maguigad, "The Unlikely Rise of Malört as Chicago's Drink," episode of *Curious City* (podcast), WBEZ, July 6, 2023, https://www.wbez.org/stories/why-is-malort-popular-in-chicago/9d45cf2d -ded9-4d48-ac88-40b7e6ed2172.

"There's no way Chicago": Ashok Selvam, "Drake Thinks He's Too Good for Malört," *Eater*, July 6, 2023, https://chicago.eater.com/2023/7/6/23786310 /drake-tries-malort-chicago-bitter-alcohol.

Media, of course, pounced: Dante, "Drake Had the Audacity to Shit Talk Malort While in Chicago," *Barstool Sports*, July 6, 2023, https://www.barstoolsports .com/blog/3473155/drake-had-the-audacity-to-shit-talk-malort-while-in -chicago; Selvam, "Drake Thinks He's Too Good."

A Reddit thread sprang up: Vinnymeow, "Even Drake Hates Malört," Reddit, July 6, 2023, https://www.reddit.com/r/PaymoneyWubby/comments/14s4d4p /even_drake_hates_mal%C3%B6rt/.

AUTHOR INTERVIEWS

Conducted between December 2021 and February 2024; italics indicate multiple interviews.

Terry Alexander
Doug Anderson
Anne-Marie Andreasson-Hogg
David Arnold
Tremaine Atkinson
Ryan Bastianelli
Pat Berger
Ed Blandford
Brad Bolt
David Brode
Sandra Brode
Taylor Brode
Mark Brown
Chris Depa
Gregory Diemond
Jeff Donahue
Emily Clark Ehrenberg
Matt Eisler
Robbie Ellis
Brenton Engel
Pat Gabelick
Owen Gibler
John Giovanazzi
Jason Griffin
Robby Haynes
Paul Hletko
Hunter Hobbs
Johnny Ice
Greg Jacobi
Dave Jemilo
Charles Joly
John Laffler
Kevin Leonard
Toby Maloney
Scott Martin

Paul McGee
Bill McGrath
Sam Mechling
Adam Melberth
Chris Mitchell
Mike Moreno
Pat Odon
Bill O'Donaghue
Patrick O'Neil
Mark Peters
Mike Polino
Archie Powell
Chandra Ram
Katherine Raz
Michael Riddet
Michael Roper
Sazerac Company representative
     (anonymity granted by request)
Jeff Schecter
Danny Shapiro
Carolyn Sievert
Robert Simonson
Anthony Spina
Randy Stoller
Peter Strom
Mike Sula
Diana Termine
Marty Tomszak
Tony Uzzardo
Brian Vaughan
Peter Vestinos
Wyl Villacres
Sam Wurth
Tyrus Yamagiwa

INDEX

ABOUT THE AUTHOR

JOSH NOEL is the author of *Barrel-Aged Stout and Selling Out: Goose Island, Anheuser-Busch, and How Craft Beer Became Big Business*, which was named best book by the North American Guild of Beer Writers in 2018. He wrote about beer and travel for the *Chicago Tribune* for over a decade, and previously covered crime and violence for the *Tribune* and other publications. He lives in Chicago with his wife and children and is at work on his next book.